SECOND EDITION

HUMANITIES TWO
Interactive

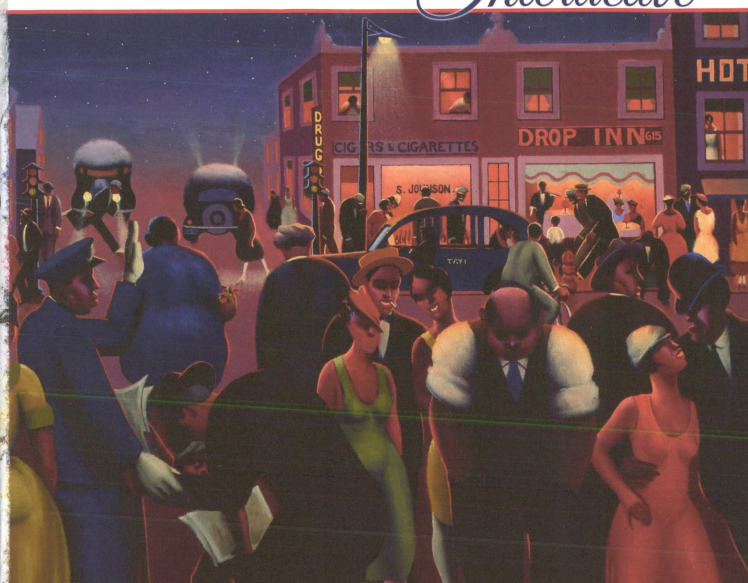

A CUSTOMIZED VERSION OF
HUMANITIES ACROSS THE ARTS BY STEPHEN HUSARIK
DESIGNED SPECIFICALLY FOR HUMANITIES 202 AT HAMPTON UNIVERSITY

Edited by **DR. KAREN TURNER WARD**

Preface by **KWABENA AMPOFO-ANTI** AND
TRACY SPENCER-STONESTREET

Kendall Hunt
publishing company

Cover design by Drs. Jacqueline F. Bontemps and Joseph Martin.

Cover Photo: Archibald Motley, *Black Belt*, 1934, Oil on canvas, 33" × 40 ½". Collection of Hampton University Museum. Copyright © Hampton University Museum. Reprinted by permission.

Kendall Hunt
publishing company

Send all inquiries to:
4050 Westmark Drive
Dubuque, IA 52004-1840

CONTENTS

Preface VII

Illustrations and Sound Files XI

Chapter 1: Humanities: Structural Approach 1

    Introduction 1

    Critical Method Steps 2

    Critical Method Application 5

    Art: An Operational Definition 5

    Humanities: An Operational Definition 8

    Folk Art vs. Urban Art 9

Chapter 2: Painting 13

    Introduction 13

    Elements of Design 15

    Principles of Design 21

    Analyzing Designs 32

    Critical Method Application 37

    Critical Terms 39

    Review Question 40

Chapter 3: Sculpture 41

    Introduction 41

    Types of Sculpture 42

    Six Sculptural Methods 45

    Elements of Design 50

Principles of Design 54

Critical Method Application 62

Critical Terms 63

Review Question 63

Chapter 4: Architecture 65

Introduction 65

Types of Architecture 66

Elements of Architecture 68

Six Architectural Techniques 70

Critical Method Application 91

Critical Terms 92

Review Question 94

Commentary 94

Chapter 5: Music 95

Introduction 95

Elements of Music 97

Critical Method Application 114

Critical Terms 114

Review Question 116

Commentary 116

Chapter 6: Literature: Lyric / Epic 117

Types of Poetry 117

Critical Method Application 137

Critical Terms 138

Review Question 139

Commentary 139

Chapter 7: Drama 141

Introduction 141

Origins of Drama 143

Elements of Drama 147

Structure of Plot 148

Oedipus Rex (Who Am I?) 149

Critical Method Application 154

Critical Terms 155

Review Question 155

Commentary 156

Chapter 8: Dance 157

Introduction 157

Types of Dance 158

Elements of Dance 160

Ballet 160

Critical Method Application 164

Critical Terms 164

Review Question 166

Commentary 166

Chapter 9: Film 167

Introduction 167

Types of Film 168

Elements of Film 169

Critical Method Application 181

Critical Terms 181

Review Question 182

Commentary 183

PREFACE

Welcome to Humanities 202. This course is a partner course to Humanities 201, in which you studied ancient civilizations, medieval culture, and the flowering of European culture in the Renaissance. We will be continuing our investigations into **culture** and **human expression** by examining specific methods of **cultural production**. As you discovered in Humanities 201, **culture** is the set of beliefs, morals, and practices that bind people together within a society. Cultures often maintain continental, political, or regional borders, but can also be as small as a college campus or town (although these smaller groups are typically called sub-cultures). Culture in the abstract—as beliefs, morals, and practices—is intangible and therefore hard to examine and study in and of itself; however, **cultural production**—the arts, crafts, music, literature, and technology of a particular culture—*is* tangible. We can derive critical knowledge about a culture by examining the creative and material output of its members.

How does a specific quilt by an African American artist inform us about the history and experience of African American society? How also does a contemporary Hollywood film reflect the beliefs and desires of 21st century America? These are the types of engaging questions you will be able to answer by the end of this course. Although this textbook will focus on Western culture, the terms, methodologies, and concepts are applicable to non-Western cultures, as well. In fact, much of what you will study this semester has roots outside Europe and the Mediterranean, as artists, musicians, playwrights, and philosophers have often found inspiration through their international travels and appreciation of other cultures.

Students in this course are encouraged to make connections between their areas of specialization and Humanities and not make the mistake of thinking that Humanities does not pertain to their field of study or career. Arts and Culture are inextricably linked to many diverse areas of study such as mathematics, science, communication, medicine, and journalism. Recognize yourself as a shaper and participant in the defining and making of culture. Appreciating the far-reaching impact of culture will enhance your ability to relate to and enjoy people and unique practices and expressions around you.

Studying the Humanities **enhances knowledge** of other disciplines in two fundamental ways. First, it teaches you in-depth methods of observation and analysis that strengthen your understanding of any subject. Second, it stretches your understanding of how and where your discipline overlaps and influences other professions. This expanded understanding of your field will help you find not only your place within it, but also areas for innovation and scholarly exploration.

The second benefit of studying the Humanities is how it will **improve communication** with people throughout your life. By studying other cultures, you will understand the customs and cultural references of your coworkers or clients from a different region or country, and will be able to share ideas and converse with them in an informed manner.

Finally, the study of Humanities **enriches experiences** for you personally. Going to plays, orchestral concerts, and art museums should be enjoyable aspects of your life; this course will give you the tools and analytical skills necessary to demonstrate an understanding and appreciation of visual and performing arts. An essential aspect of a college-educated adult is having visual and cultural literacy: viewing, discussing and evaluating creative output.

Aesthetics, the concern for beauty or physical appearance, plays a major part in the study of Humanities, especially the visual arts and architecture. The study of aesthetics goes hand in hand with the study of creative production. Even though you may not realize it, you are already using many of the tools of creative production every day. From choosing what to wear, to posting and editing images on Instagram, to making decisions about how to arrange your furniture, you are actively participating in aesthetic and cultural production all the time. Let this give you confidence: you already have the basic tools for understanding and evaluating art, music, architecture, drama, and more. As you navigate your way in this course, consider how the concepts you are learning can be applied to your everyday life.

Hampton University's rich cultural heritage enhances our in-depth study of creative production in several ways. First, an understanding of architecture, art, theatre, music, and dance provides you with a deeper appreciation for the historical and creative significance of our buildings, murals, and world-class Hampton University Museum. It also enriches your experience of the many theatrical performances, dance, and musical concerts available each semester. Second, your education will be buttressed by firsthand experiences, as you attend these events as part of this class's requirements. The ability to observe firsthand a theatrical performance—to experience the lights, set, and dramatic dialogue—is to witness the transformation of the written word into lived experience. Through class discussions and written assignments, you will gain direct experience analyzing cultural events. Finally, Hampton University's strong relationship with the community at large through its art exhibitions, performances, and creative lecture series demonstrates the ability of art to serve as community outreach and continued education. Through your experiences in this class, you will see how far-reaching and significant the impact of the arts can be.

The structure of Humanities 202 is interactive and thematic. We will use the textbook, online resources, and campus activities to explore different modes of cultural production. This textbook offers a thematic approach to the arts, meaning that we will focus on one method of creative production at a time. A singular focus on painting, sculpture, architecture, music, literature, dance, drama, and film allows you to understand concepts and trends specific to one discipline at a time, and to have the opportunity to apply methods of critical analysis to individual works of art. This method also prepares you for a lifetime of art appreciation and understanding. The course content is enriched and solidified through the online portion of the textbook. Online activities, such as games, case studies, quizzes, and exams, will enhance classroom lectures and discussions, and will help you guarantee your understanding of important concepts, methods of inquiry, and key figures. This course will also use the various cultural events at Hampton University as primary resources in your understanding of cultural production; theatrical performances, art gallery receptions, musical concerts, and thought-provoking lectures will give you firsthand experience in using the tools of cultural analysis and evaluation.

On completion of this course, with your realization of the dynamic nature of culture and your ability to look, listen, and interpret, you will be empowered by your knowledge to build bridges of understanding and appreciation across cultures. A lasting engagement with the humanistic tradition will greatly help you embark on life's journey knowing and living *education for life*—a motto for every true Hamptonian.

Ms. Tracy Spencer-Stonestreet and Mr. Kwabena Ampofo-Anti

ILLUSTRATIONS AND SOUND FILES

Unless otherwise indicated in the Credits section, photos in this text were taken by Stephen Husarik. A debt of thanks is owed to: Darren Rainey for the musical compositions that accompany Chapter 5, Steffi Wiggins and Britt Morrison for the screenplay in Chapter 9, and Colin McClain and Raechel Martin for their graphic illustrations.

HUMANITIES: STRUCTURAL APPROACH

INTRODUCTION

What you can you tell about the object shown in Figure **1.1**? Do you know anything about its origin? Can you determine if someone made it? Does it call any associations to mind? These are especially difficult questions because the object appears to be inert stone or concrete broken away from a larger object and people typically do not have associations with unidentified fragments of inert materials.

One might try to describe the object and its roots: it has a broken edge and a smooth semicircular side that may have been formed in a cast; it must weigh a great deal per unit volume because it is made of rock aggregate and granular cement particles; formed concrete of this type must come from an advanced society, etc., etc. Such an investigation could go on endlessly and we still might not ever know if the object has importance.

If you are told that this is a piece of the Berlin Wall, however, you may have much more to say about it. A seemingly inert object suddenly takes on meaning and releases constellations of information associated with a particular historical period. In this case, the object is part of a wall that stretched over ninety miles separating two societies during the Cold War following World War II. The Berlin Wall inspired many stories about political espionage and people's attempts to escape from the Soviet Union into the West. The wall conjures up stories about the general fear of the Soviets as a world nuclear power during the 1960s, and even the remarkable day in 1987 when President Ronald Reagan asked Prime Minister Gorbachev to "tear down this wall." One might even discuss the day the Berlin Wall fell in October 1989 and how Beethoven's Symphony No. 9 was performed nearby to celebrate the fall of this last vestige of the old Soviet order.

So it is with objects illustrated in this textbook. Some of them may be familiar and others may be totally new. Some may immediately suggest topics of conversation and others may suggest nothing at all.

In order to discuss objects about which you are unfamiliar, you will need a method of inquiry based upon years of tested debate, discussion, and experience. The method adapted here comes from principles found in Benjamin Bloom's Taxonomy,* and is labeled the "Critical Method."

CRITICAL METHOD STEPS

Bloom's treatise gives many examples of the ways in which we learn and methods for examining the world around us. A number of those principles are selected and paraphrased below in order to increase your efficiency in thinking about artworks. The steps include Description, Analysis, Interpretation, and Evaluation.

Source: Steven Husarik

FIGURE 1.1

© Album/Joseph Martin/Album/SuperStock; Cubo Images/Cubo Images

FIGURE 1.2 *The Starry Night* (1889), Vincent van Gogh. Museum of Modern Art, New York

*Bloom, Benjamin, *Taxonomy of Educational Objectives: The Classification of Educational Goals; Handbook I: Cognitive Domain* (New York: Longmans, Green, 1956), 201–207.

DESCRIPTION

In this step, one describes the object, everything known about it and what it looks like. It is important to give the title, the creator's name, the date, the type of media, its function, and its location.

ANALYSIS

This an important skill developed throughout this Humanities textbook. In analysis, things are taken apart and assessed according to standards. For example, in literature one can analyze a work in terms of its plot, character, symbols, setting, and point of view. Knowing and applying critical terms to art works is central in gaining insight about them.

INTERPRETATION

In this step, themes are brought together and patterns are identified. The result may be an essay, a commentary, a research paper, or simply a conversation. Patterns are arranged in new ways and discussed in order to understand various levels of meaning. What is the significance of this object? What ideas does it present? How are its meanings and content expressed as patterns?

EVALUATION

This final step involves an appraisal of previous information. Where does this specific object belong in our world? How does it reflect other things at the same time in history? If it is part of a larger piece, where does it belong and what influence does it have? Does it have a place in history? Is it possible to develop a personal point of view about this object?

These four steps can be applied to seemingly inert objects such as the Berlin Wall fragment shown in Figure **1.1** or to art works that are obviously charged with meaning such as *The Starry Night* (1889) by Vincent van Gogh shown in Figure **1.2**. Please read the Critical Method given for this famous painting and add observations to the discussion.

DESCRIPTION

The Starry Night (1889) by Vincent van Gogh (1853–1890) is an oil on canvas (29" x 36 ¼") showing a cypress tree in a landscape, with a village, distant mountains, and swirling abstract representations of clouds in the sky (Figure **1.2**). Van Gogh is known to have produced designs similar to this with slightly contorted images and choppy brush strokes that are said to reflect his inner psychological struggle. The painting shows the night at sky in Saint-Remy, France where the artist was staying in a hospital. It may actually document stars in the sky that night.

INTERPRETATION

The painting aims to capture the spirit of the night sky in southern France. Since the stars are represented larger than they actually appear, it may be possible to assign symbolic significance to them. However this would require a careful review of the artist's statements or correspondence with his brother in order to arrive at a correct interpretation. *The Starry Night* forces one to abandon traditional principles of visual depiction and incorporate alternative methods of artistic criticism; the agitated brush strokes suggest a new avenue into how an artist can create images by superimposing interesting textures.

ANALYSIS

The Starry Night dominates in the use of a blue hue—suggestive of nighttime scenes—and it subordinates in green and yellow hues. Objects are simplified to their basic outlines and appear cartoon-like because primary colors (blue, yellow) dominate. The colors consist of opaque paint pigments (impasto) rather than traditional transparent oil glazes and the surface texture is agitated with continuous splotches of paint that relate to the artist's passion for his subject. This painting is "open" and "painterly," to use art historian Heinrich Wölfflin's terminology (see Chapter 1, Figures **1.29–1.30**). Its unity is achieved by a dominating blue color, a dense surface texture, and the repetition of organic shapes. Asymmetrical in structure, the painting employs photographic proportion. Although an argument could be made for the presence of atmospheric perspective, this painting appears essentially flat because of its noticeable surface texture. Stuttering brush strokes, contorted images and a strange night setting aside, the painting has a very pleasant color scheme resulting from the use of analogous colors (see color wheel, Chapter 1, Figure **1.12**).

FIGURE 1.3 Detail, *The Starry Night* (1889), Vincent van Gogh. Museum of Modern Art, New York

© Album/Joseph Martin/Album/SuperStock; Cubo Images/Cubo Images

CRITICAL METHOD APPLICATION

The Critical Method presented here is suitable for any art object and could be applied to single artworks such as van Gogh's *The Starry Night*, or whole genres of artworks. Criticism in this form can be done by one person, or by a group of people working as a team. When employed by groups of people, the Critical Method may result in perceptive case studies on even the most complex subjects. Now that you have had an opportunity to review the Critical Method applied to Gogh's *The Starry Night* you can use it as a model for the application of the Critical Method for any art object.

ART: AN OPERATIONAL DEFINITION

Imagine yourself sitting on a chair in a classroom. Is the chair art? Some people will immediately respond "no," and others will say "yes." While sitting in chairs, most of us probably do not think of chairs as art because they have a functional purpose—to hold us up in a seated position.

FIGURE 1.4 Chair Standing on One Leg

If a chair is tilted upon just one leg and mounted on a pedestal in a museum (see Figure **1.4**), however, would people consider it art? Possibly they would. As visitors walk by, the chair looks very amusing standing on just one leg. It invites inspection because a chair does not normally stand on one leg alone; it may remind some visitors of the times they sat in similar chairs. Perhaps if someone sees gum pasted underneath the seat that may cause them to remember times they pasted gum underneath chairs themselves, or the times when they wrote something on the attached desk, or listened to people in an auditorium rattling on about subjects of no interest to them. Visitors to the museum are thus engaged with the chair. Once they are engaged—with all the memories and associations the object brings—they are participating in the artistic experience.

The chair has become art, by our definition, because it is a manmade object that awakens memories or associations. With this definition in mind, one can understand why the block of concrete presented in Figure **1.1** does not qualify as art; most observers would probably treat it as an inert fragment.

This definition of art may have both positive and negative consequences—especially when it is applied to celebrated art works from the past. For example, a naïve patron may enter the Louvre Museum in Paris and easily walk by the *Mona Lisa* without having any interest in the painting. If that person knows nothing about the painting, they could ignore and disregard one of the most famous paintings of all time. The art object sends out information, but the viewer does not receive it. By our definition, an art object has to stir up associations and provoke interest in order to be labeled art. It has to engage the viewer in some way. If it does not engage, it might be art for some people, but not for the unengaged.

Perhaps if the viewer knows something about Leonardo's painting—that the *Mona Lisa* was one of the few paintings ever stolen from the Louvre museum—that the Roman bridge behind Mona's shoulder was recently identified as being in Lecco, Italy—that the design is riddled with sequences of parabolas—and that the sitter's famous smile is inscribed perfectly within the vertex of a parabola, then the painting might hold some interest. It might even engage the viewer and awaken memories or associations. In that case, it would become art.

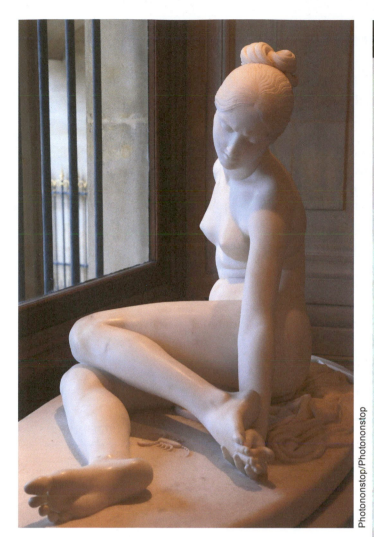

FIGURE 1.5 *Nymph with Scorpion* (ca. 1826), Lorenzo
Bartolini (1777–1850). Musée Condé, Chantilly, France

Photononstop/Photononstop

NUDE VS. NAKED

Do you think the figure illustrated in Figure **1.5** is naked? If so, please read on. In 1956, the celebrated art historian Sir Kenneth Clark published a book entitled *The Nude: A Study in Ideal Form* (Doubleday Anchor). In the preface, he explained the reasoning behind his book's title. Clark wrote that terms such as "naked" do not allow us to describe and evaluate artworks objectively because they cloud our judgments with distractions. He understood the power of associations.

Consider the following situation: someone has just told you that they have a painting of a naked lady hanging over their fireplace. Does this create distracting thoughts in your mind? Consider an alternative situation: someone has just told you that they have a painting of a nude hanging over their fireplace. Is your thought process distracted now? A neutral term such as "nude" avoids distracting associations. This example illustrates the power of words to influence thought.

The neutral term "nude" will be used throughout this text to refer to any artwork depicting a person not wearing clothes in order to ensure objectivity in our evaluations and help us avoid distracting associations.

Historically speaking the word art has many definitions. There are the arts of the French academy, the arts of Africa, China, and the art of Pop Culture from America. Much space could be devoted to the explanation of historical definitions and situations where the term art occurs, but that would convert this text into to the branch of philosophy known as Aesthetics. In order to expedite our arts survey, therefore, this text offers an operational definition broad enough to encompass most things that people call art today. Art is here defined as manmade objects that awaken memories or associations.

HUMANITIES: AN OPERATIONAL DEFINITION

Humanities may be defined as criticism that deals with the arts, but it also includes any field of historical research. *Humanities Across the Arts* is a survey and study of criticism about Western culture in terms of artistic artifacts. Artistic artifacts may include objects such as paintings, pieces of music, sculpture, buildings, or even soda bottles if they identify places, designs, and materials from a specific culture (e.g., 20th century industrial designs constructed of glass, plastic, and aluminum). These artifacts help define the object of our study, Western culture.

Culture refers to a group of people who live a particular lifestyle and/or hold similar beliefs and values. Most cultures are located in a particular time or place; however, some cultures are polyglot and cover disparate geographical areas. Western culture, for example, is a set of ideas, values, and beliefs from the Ancient Greek world that have been preserved over more than twenty-five centuries—through many languages—in Europe and America. Many of these ideas and attitudes currently reside within readers of this book. As an historical concept, Western culture is best explained by considering the timeline below:

TIMELINE OF WESTERN CULTURE

ANCIENT GREECE	RENAISSANCE	POST MODERN ERA
5TH CENT. B.C.E.————	1450–1600 C.E.————————	2000 C.E.—————————

B.C.E. = Before the Common Era   C.E. = Common Era

About twenty-five centuries ago (500 B.C.E.—five hundred years Before the Common Era), a culture flourished in Ancient Greece that marked the beginning of Western culture. It was one of the earliest cultures to place a high value on individuals, the first to distribute power equitably among its citizens, and one of the first to use rotating civil governments. The Ancient Greeks developed the idea of a contract between citizens and government, invented our modern musical scale (*do, re, mi, fa, sol, etc.*) and even invented the word "atom." The list of their achievements in the arts, sciences, and mathematics is considerable.

Some twenty centuries later, during the Renaissance, there was an attempt to revive the writings and ideas of the Ancient Romans based upon an admiration of Ancient Greek writers. The movement was labeled in Italian as *Rinascimento* and is now popularly known by the French word *Renaissance*— meaning "Rebirth" or "Born Again" (Naissance means birth, and Renaissance means rebirth). Italian scholars didn't want to be like the Ancient Greeks; they wanted to be Ancient Greeks. They wanted to understand the key features that made the Ancient Greeks great and return to that way of thinking and acting. Their attitude was embodied in a program of study called *studia humanitatis* (i.e. The Study of Humanities).

Renaissance scholars proceeded to uncover the ideas of the Ancient Greeks by translating written documents, excavating temples and statuary, and even imitating the designs of ancient architecture. Eventually, they understood that Ancient Greek greatness was connected to "Humanism," which translates essentially as individualism, or placing importance on individuals. The theory holds that we are all important as individuals, if for no other reason than each of us is a walking database of individual experiences. Each of us is unique and worth knowing for our individuality and that alone contributes to the betterment of society.

Today, Humanities is an extension of that old Renaissance study, and in many schools around the country it is a study of how individualism is surviving. In this particular text, however, Humanities is treated as a form of arts criticism that uncovers facts about culture and offers perspectives on the way people of the past viewed the world. The artwork is the central focus of our study.

FOLK ART VS. URBAN ART

Artworks are very effective sources for the study of culture and values. This potential aspect of art to reveal cultural attitudes often appeals to students more than the actual study of artworks themselves. A value is something that a particular group of people feels is important. Artworks can reveal cultural values and tell us about people, their aspirations, and their world outlooks. Knowing what other people value, and how they think, helps us understand our own point of view and to find our own way in the world.

FIGURE 1.6 Folk Society

Source: Steven Husarik

FOLK ART

Imagine an old sepia-tinted photograph (Figure **1.6**). In the center, a man sits on a chair and has a stern look on his face. A woman stands next to him with a restrained smile on her face. Young people of different sizes, ages, and genders are sitting and standing around them and everyone is dressed in Sunday-best outfits. They are standing in front of what looks like a farm house constructed of simple planks. Next to the people, on the right side (not visible in the photo), a large iron wheel protrudes into the photo. It is a piece of farm machinery. On the left side of the photo (also not visible), one can imagine farmland behind the house where someone has been working the soil, and mountains that appear in the far distance. This is may be farm family, perhaps located in the heartland of America. What do you think would be important to the people in this photograph? What would they value most?

FOLK VALUES

SURVIVAL SKILLS	RELIGION	FRUGALITY	HARD WORK	FAMILY

This farm family can serve as a model for a folk society. It is difficult to live on a farm and these people place a high value on food, clothing, and basic survival skills. Frugality and hard work are important to them and they need everyone they can get to help, so the family unit is important. They probably would not want party-loving neighbors living down the road; they need dependable, reliable folks who can help out in an emergency.

FOLK ARTS

WORK SONGS	TOOL-MAKING	WEAPON DESIGNS	RELIGIOUS ICONS	FOLK DANCES

What kind of art do people in a folk society typically favor? People in this environment typically place a high value on useful or utilitarian art. If they have tools, they put carvings on them; if they have weapons they may put designs on the handles. Since religion is important to them, they may possess religious icons. Since they can't afford to have a full symphony orchestra playing while they are working the fields, they sing work songs to pass the time, and engage in folk dances for entertainment.

URBAN ART

Compare the lifestyle and values of folk societies with those of complex societies in an urban setting. In an all-electric complex society materialism, personal possessions and pleasure are important. One need only look around to see computers, laptops, electronic watches on people's arms today—to see gold necklaces on people's necks, and to hear people talking on cell phones. Materialism is present everywhere in our modern, complex society. You may be reading this Humanities text in conjunction with an online course, sitting in front of an expensive computer, or carrying a mobile device while driving to school listening to music produced with synthesizers. Complex societies typically place a high value on individualism and also place a high value on career identity.

URBAN VALUES

MATERIALISM	POSSESSIONS	LUXURIES	INDIVIDUAL	CAREER IDENTITY

What kind of art do people in a complex society like? They like the kinds of art listed as the first eight chapters of this book—the fine arts. Someone might say, "Well, I'm a member of a complex society and I don't particularly care for those arts and I'm not especially good at judging them."

FINE ARTS

PAINTING	SCULPTURE	ARCHITECTURE	MUSIC	LITERATURE	DANCE	DRAMA	FILM

Are you sure? Are the walls in your home absolutely bare, with no pictures or wallpaper on them? Have you never selected a greeting card with verse in it? Do you not like music? Young married couples spend endless hours haggling over the traffic patterns in their new or rehabbed house trying to decide where an extra bathroom will be located, or where the children's rooms should be located. Do you not think they are aware of space planning and architecture? Certainly everyone goes to movie theaters to see films—it's the most popular of all modern art forms. Do you not comment about movies you see to other people? It is the goal of this text to explain the meaning and function of these art forms and their connection to you and your life in general.

PAINTING

"Have no fear of perfection, you'll never reach it."
—Salvador Dali (1904-1989)

INTRODUCTION

Two paintings are shown here; one is the *Death of Socrates* (Figure **2.1**), by Jacques-Louis David, and the other is *Seamless abstract geometric colorful vector pattern for continuous* replicate (Figure **2.2**), by Fedorov Oleksiy. How would the average person discuss these paintings if they were placed side-by-side? Someone might speculate about the people in the David painting and develop a narrative for it, but then what would someone say about the Oleksiy design? Is there a story to go with that?

Modern artists do not necessarily create stories to go with paintings. More often, they employ critical terms known as elements and principles of design to describe their paintings. Virtually every art form has its own elements and principles.

FIGURE 2.1 *Death of Socrates* (1787), Jacques-Louis David. Metropolitan Museum of Art, New York

FIGURE 2.2 *Seamless abstract geometric colorful vector pattern for continuous replicate,* Fedorov Oleksiy

Knowing these terms and their definitions enables a spectator to discuss both David's and Olevksiy's designs on the same level. The elements of art—value, shape, line, texture, and color—are explained in the following discussion.

ELEMENTS OF DESIGN

VALUE

Ernest Cialone, 2007. Courtesy of the artist.

FIGURE 2.3 *The Discipline of Mirth* (2007), Ernest Cialone. University of Arkansas – Fort Smith

highlight

core shadow

half tone

© National Gallery, London / Art Resource, NY

FIGURE 2.4 Detail, *Angel*, from *Madonna of the Rocks* (1495–1508), Leonardo da Vinci. London, National Gallery

Value is defined as black, white, and all degrees of gray in between. One can observe various degrees of lightness and darkness in the drawing by Ernest Cialone (Figure **2.3**). The artist has rendered numerous areas of the juggler's outfit in light and dark to reveal how light and shadow combine to form the image of the subject. Black occurs in the shadows, white in the highlights, and other gray tones in between.

A special use of value produces three-dimensional qualities known as *chiaroscuro*. *Chiaroscuro* is an Italian word that refers to the contrast between light and dark in rounded objects—especially in flesh tones. In the detail of Figure **2.4** from Leonardo da Vinci's *Madonna of the Rocks* one can immediately see a strong contrast between light and dark on the angel's rounded cheek. Three properties are necessary to achieve a rounded effect with *chiaroscuro*: 1) a highlighted area that is separated from 2) an area of half tone 3) with a dark core shadow in between. The highlight is easily visible on this angel's face, as well as the dark core shadow under her cheekbone, and a lighter gray tone of reflected light that can be observed beneath. *Chiaroscuro* is one way to depict spatial qualities in an image.

SHAPE

Shape may be defined as an enclosed area of space defined by lines or color contrasts. Both geometric and organic shapes are usually present in an image.

Geometric Shapes

Geometric shapes include the circle, square, triangle, rectangle, oval, and so forth. One often finds paintings with purely geometrical designs in 20th century art (Figure **2.5**) or in decorative folk art and non-Western cultures. These shapes are also present in the design of architecture.

FIGURE 2.5 *Homage to the Square: Apparition* (1959), Josef Albers. Guggenheim Museum, New York

FIGURE 2.6 *Personages with Stars* (1933), Joan Miró. Art Institute of Chicago, Chicago

Organic Shapes

Organic shapes are necessary for the depiction of photographic reality. They result from the combination of curves and angles and often fall into families or groups. Some painters spend much time learning to render organic shapes so they can accurately portray faces, bodies, landscapes, and so forth in their naturalistic works. Organic shapes are useful in themselves to create interesting and unified abstract designs as in Joan Miró's painting *Personages with Stars* (1933) that presents many variations of a single organic shape (Figure **2.6**). Since there are no common names for individual organic shapes, or for families of organic shapes, one might say that the main motif for Miró's painting is a "dog bone shape," even though the artist never assigned that catch phrase to his artwork.

LINE

In mathematics, a line is defined as a connection between two points, but in design it is necessary to carry the distinction further with expressed line (sometimes-called "actual" line) and implied line.

Expressed (Actual) Line

One can easily see expressed lines in a drawing, etching, or engraving. When a pencil or pen point is pressed onto a piece of paper, the resulting line(s) may be thick, thin, or full of variations. Variation in thickness and thinness of lines determines whether the viewer perceives three-dimensional objects or flat pattern designs.

The characters illustrated in Leonardo da Vinci's silverpoint drawing *Five Grotesque Heads* (Figure **2.7**) have lost their teeth, the tone of their facial muscles, and all other signs of youthful beauty. They are not beautiful as individuals, but the drawing itself is beautiful because of the great variety of thick and thin lines.

Notice the manner in which Leonardo defines the shapes of these grotesque heads through a cunning use of line. Sometimes the lines are thick, sometimes thin, and sometimes they appear as rows of parallel lines (hatchings) that give the impression of shadow. Shadows are even more pronounced when the parallel lines cross each other at 90 degrees angles (cross-hatchings). It is said that an artist is a great draughtsman when s/he can define objects with as few lines as possible.

Implied Line

Implied lines result from the juxtaposition of color/value shapes against one another. Most viewers perceive that Fernand Legér's *Mural Painting* (Figure **2.8**) has a linear quality, but there are very few actual lines in the painting. Most of the lines result from shapes with hard edges that touch each other. The hard edges of shapes in contrasting colors are sufficient to give the idea that lines are present even though they are not. The observer's eye traces the line quality on the edge of the shapes.

FIGURE 2.7 *Five Grotesque Heads* (1494), Leonardo da Vinci. Windsor Collection, Royal Library, London

FIGURE 2.8 *Mural painting (1924)*, Fernand Legér. Museum of Modern Art, New York

Numerous tools have been devised for placing lines on paper, papyrus, and other materials over the centuries. Paintbrushes and/or ink-dipped pens were used to create ancient papyrus mockup drawings for the walls of Egyptian tombs. Renaissance artists used *silverpoint* to make portraits by pulling a silver wire into a pen-holder and drawing in the manner of a modern pencil. Pencils, invented in the 1800s, are made of graphite and clay pressed into a wooden holder. Conte crayons are a highly flexible wax-based medium that, if sharpened to a microscopically sharp point, are highly flexible media for drawing. They can be used on the surfaces of Bavarian limestone to create almost photographic *lithographs*. Finally, *intaglio* is a form of drawing where an image is created by cutting, carving, or engraving onto a flat surface. *Etching* (with acid) enhances this process by adding depth and character to the cut.

TEXTURE

Texture is defined as the density of pattern on surfaces. There are two types of texture in flat pattern design, surface texture, and visual texture.

Surface (Tactile) Texture

Surface texture is texture that can be felt with the sense of touch. If one were to rub one's fingers against a concrete wall, it has a rough surface texture—even though the wall might appear as smooth from a distance. Rough surface textures are found in most paintings by Vincent van Gogh (Figure **2.9**) because the artist dabbed globs of paint onto the surface of his canvases. Running fingers across these surfaces would result in a rough sensation to the touch. Of course, no one should never touch a painting because oil from the fingertips would leave marks that oxidize and later turn the artwork dark.

Visual Texture

Visual texture concerns the subdivision of space in terms of shape and value; it is essentially a design issue. Peter Paul Rubens' paintings are good examples of rough (or dense) visual texture. Although these paintings are glazed with varnish many times over, and their surfaces are smooth to the touch, they typically contain thousands of contrasting shapes that create the effect of dense visual texture because the design is broken into tiny shapes.

In Ruben's painting entitled *Fall of the Damned* (Figure **2.10**), thousands of organic shapes in the background and muscles of the figures break up the space of the design. Even though its surface texture is smooth, this painting has a rough (or dense) visual texture. Many of the figures in this painting appear to have rough surfaces on them that depict lumpy fat and muscles. Actually, these depicted surfaces are composed of numerous organic shapes. Sometimes the concepts of visual texture and surface texture get confused when critics refer to the "rough surfaces" on objects in a painting: what is meant is that the depicted objects create a dense visual texture.

COLOR

Color is a high band frequency in the visual spectrum that includes the concepts of *hue* and *saturation*. A popular misconception is that colors are perceived as warm and/or cool. In the color wheel shown in Figure **2.12**, colors having a lower frequency (*e.g.*, yellow) are alleged to possess a warmer temperature than those with a higher frequency (*e.g.*, blue). Colors do not have temperatures. We associate fire or heat with

FIGURE 2.9 A stamp depicting Vincent van Gogh.

yellow and red, and cool water and the sky with green and blue, but the connection is only associational and not real.

Hue

Hue is the name of the color itself, for example red, blue, or green. The hue of the stout harlequin's outfit in the painting shown in Figure **2.11** by Pablo Picasso is red.

FIGURE 2.10 *Fall of the Damned* (1620), Peter Paul Rubens. Alte Pinakothek, Munich

FIGURE 2.11 *Family of Saltimbanques* (1905), Pablo Picasso. National Gallery of Art, Washington, D.C.

Saturation

Saturation refers to the amount of color present in any given color patch. The ballerina's pink outfit in Picasso's *Family of Saltimbanques* in Figure **2.11** has low saturation. We can see that pink is present in the image, but it appears rather grayish. The more color that is present in a depicted object, the higher is its saturation; the grayer an object looks, the lower its color saturation. In general, there is a strong presence of blue in Claude Monet's *Water Lilies* (Figure **2.13**), and so the painting has a high saturation of blue.

COLOR WHEEL

In addition to hue and saturation, two commonly used terms in discussing paintings are complementary and analogous colors. Isaac Newton, Johann von Goethe, Hermann von Helmholtz and others helped develop a color theory in the 18th and 19th centuries that resulted in an arrangement called the color wheel shown in Figure **2.12**. Colors form relationships on the wheel: two colors next to each other are said to be analogous and those opposite each other on the wheel are said to be complementary. When artists use these color relationships systematically, it contributes to the unity of their paintings.

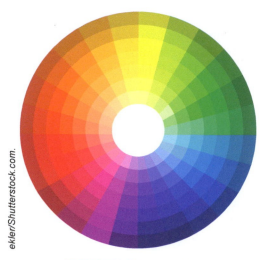

ekler/Shutterstock.com.

FIGURE 2.12 Color Wheel

Analogous [Adjacent] Colors

Analogous colors are located next to each other on the color wheel [e.g., blue-purple]. Monet's *Water Lilies* shown in Figure **2.13** is an effective example of *analogous* colors because of its use of green, blue, and purple.

Complementary Colors

Complementary colors are located opposite each other on the color wheel [e.g., blue-orange]. The pomegranate held by *Persephone* in the pre-Raphaelite painting by Daniel Gabriel Rosetti (Figure **2.14**) is orange, while her gown is blue. These complementary colors create contrast, richness, and interest in the design.

Fine Art/Getty Images

FIGURE 2.13 *Water Lilies* (1906), Claude Monet. Art Institute of Chicago, Chicago

Tate Gallery, London/Art Resource, NY

FIGURE 2.14 Detail, *Persephone* (1874), Dante Gabriel Rosetti. Tate Gallery, London

ACTIVITY

Greeting card manufacturing is a major contemporary arts industry. Break up into teams and design a greeting card on the theme of "Happy Birthday." You may wish to split your team into a writers group and a design group. Your card should include a catchy title page, meaningful internal text, and a design that uses four elements of design discussed above (identified and labeled). Both the text(s) and image(s) should be coordinated into a greeting card suitable for publication.

PRINCIPLES OF DESIGN

The elements of design are combined and manipulated into patterns to create the principles of design. Critics and artists alike know and use at least some of the following terms in their conversation and work: unity, variety, focal point, balance, scale and proportion, direction, space and perspective, open vs. closed, linear vs. painterly, sequence, *trompe l'oeil*, dominance vs. sub-ordinance, positive and negative shapes.

UNITY VS. VARIETY

Unity

Typically, a painting will have some form of unity created by the repetition of elements. The result a highly unified minimalist design; however, the same unity can be achieved in a complex design.

FIGURE 2.15 *In the Days of Sappho* (1904), John Godward. J. Paul Getty Museum, Los Angeles

FIGURE 2.16 *Portrait of a Man with a Golden Helmet,* School of Rembrandt van Rijn. Gemäldegalerie, Berlin

Variety

Disregarding all other aspects of its design, John Godward's *In the Days of Sappho* (Figure **2.15**) has much more variety in terms of its shapes than Donald Judd's painting. The numerous organic shapes of the sitter's dress, the splotches of color on the animal skin, the veins in the marble, and the leaves on the trees all combine to create thousands of unique and varied shapes. In terms of its shapes alone, this painting has great variety.

FOCAL POINT

Sometimes a painting has a focal point, or area of main interest, as in this *Portrait of a Man with a Golden Helmet* (Figure **2.16**). Possibly, this painting should be re-titled the

Portrait of a Golden Helmet with a Man, because the first thing observed is the bright spot of light on the man's helmet—a focal point. If one were to lay this painting flat on a table and view the surface, one would see small mountains of paint piled up on the canvas in the area of the helmet. The artist seems determined to direct the viewer's attention to this spot in the painting, if not by having a spot of light, then by employing a three-dimensional layering of opaque paint known by the Italian word *impasto*.

BALANCE

Balance is a perceived distribution of visual weight. There are three types of balance in painting: symmetrical, asymmetrical, and radial.

Symmetrical

When symmetrical paintings are divided in half (see dotted line), one side is a mirror image of the other—as in Salvador Dali's *St. John of the Cross* (Figure **2.17**). Symmetrical is a relative term in design, since not everything seen on one side of a painting is typically an exact mirror image of the other. The clouds at the bottom of Dali's painting and the shadow of the arm at the top are not symmetrical but, otherwise, the design is essentially the same on both the right and left side.

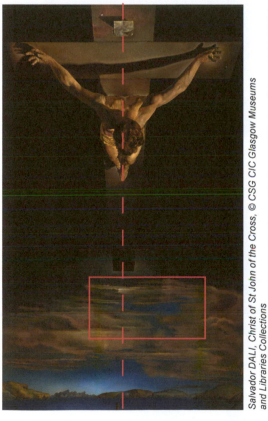

Salvador DALI, Christ of St John of the Cross, © CSG CIC Glasgow Museums and Libraries Collections

ATTACK ON ST. JOHN OF THE CROSS

Dali's painting was attacked twice by vandals. The first attack involved ripping, tearing, and considerable damage to the canvas. A close-up view of the artwork shows just how much damage needed repair. From a distance it is now difficult to see where the tear marks are located, but up close the damage is detectable. Undertaken out of necessity, this restoration was successful, but some restorations yield much less favorable results.

FIGURE 2.17 *St. John of the Cross* (1951), Salvador Dali. Kelvingrove Art Gallery and Museum, Glasgow

Asymmetrical

It is possible to create balance even though two sides of a painting have different designs as in *Arrangement in Grey and Black No. 1* (Figure **2.18**) by James McNeil Whistler. Not only is there an alignment of the depicted images on a grid, but there is a balance in the textures as well. Note how the eye is drawn to the small detailed areas in the lacework of the lady's cuff and collar on the right side; yet, there is nothing to look at on the left side of the painting except a large gray rectangle. Balance is achieved in this painting by contrasting small areas of excessive detail (i.e., lacework) with large areas of largely no interest (i.e., large rectangular curtain to the left).

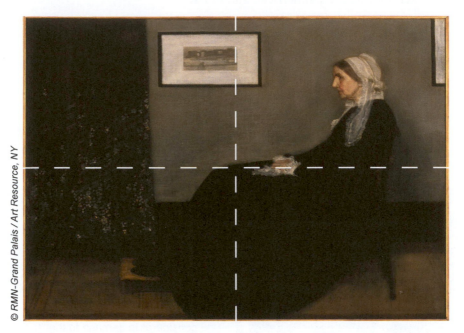

© RMN-Grand Palais / Art Resource, NY

FIGURE 2.18 *Arrangement in Grey and Black No. 1 (1871),* James McNeil Whistler. Musée d'Orsay, Paris

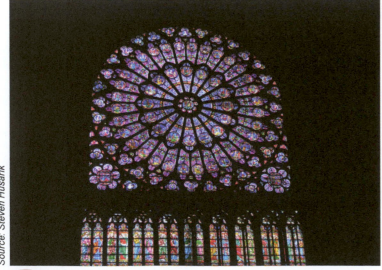

Source: Steven Husarik

Radial

Designs with radial balance show equal distribution from a center point; they are typically found in the art of world religions and in the stained-glass windows of medieval cathedrals (Figure **2.19**).

FIGURE 2.19 *South Rose window, (ca. 1260, restored, ca.1725, Guillaume Brice).* Notre-Dame Cathedral, Paris

SCALE AND PROPORTION

Scale and proportion are relative concepts. In medieval religious paintings, for example, patrons and angels often appear small in size even though they are seemingly placed in the foreground of the painting. Medieval artists painted a spiritual world exempt from the earth-bound laws of nature. Thus, the most important figures are represented as the largest. This is called hieratic scale and is discussed at the end of this chapter. In the painting of *The Virgin and Child Enthroned* (Figure **2.20**) by Cimabue, contemporary viewers expect angels, apostles, and donors in the foreground to be much larger because they are in front of Mary and Christ (photographic scale). However, since they are not as important as the central figures of Christianity, Cimabue has depicted them in a smaller size.

DIRECTION

Paintings usually present a dominant horizontal, vertical, or diagonal direction. *American Gothic* (Figure **2.21**) by Grant Wood dominates in the vertical direction. Originally titled *The Farmer's Daughter*, both the farmer and his daughter stand in stiff upright poses. Even the objects around them, such as the three-tined fork and pointed Gothic window, contribute to the sense of vertical direction.

SPACE AND PERSPECTIVE

Filippo Brunelleschi (1377–1446), was one of the earliest inventors of single point perspective that enables the viewer to perceive spatial effects on a flat surface design—giving depth to buildings just as they appear in photographs. One of the great achievements in the history of design, linear perspective had its counterpart in musical harmony. Both appeared about the same time during the Renaissance in 15th century Italy and, interestingly, both lost importance at the beginning of the 20th century. There are two principal devices that create a sense of depth in a design: 1) linear perspective and 2) atmospheric perspective.

FIGURE 2.20 *The Virgin and Child Enthroned* (*Maestà*, 1280–1285), Cimabue. Uffizi Gallery, Florence

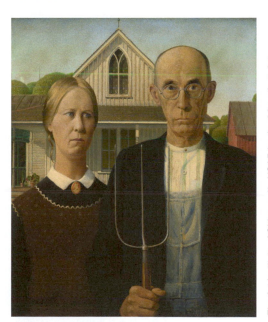

FIGURE 2.21 *American Gothic* (1930), Grant Wood.

FIGURE 2.22 *Persistence of Memory* (1932), Salvador Dali. Museum of Modern Art, New York

FIGURE 2.23 *Disintegration of the Persistence of Memory* (1952–54), Salvador, Dali. Salvador Dali Museum, St. Petersburg, Florida

Linear Perspective

Linear perspective is based upon the idea that diagonal lines converge on a single dot or collection of dots. Salvador Dali's *Disintegration of the Persistence of Memory* (1952–54) (Figure **2.23**) is made of many blocks that are positioned on lines converging on points located at the back of the painting. This is an exploded version of an earlier painting Dali did on the same subject in 1931 (Figure **2.22**); the converging lines in *Disintegration* produce an extreme sense of depth not present in the original version of the painting.

Atmospheric Perspective

Paintings can also create the impression of depth by using atmospheric perspective. In this technique, objects lose contrast and take on the color of the landscape as they fade into the distance.

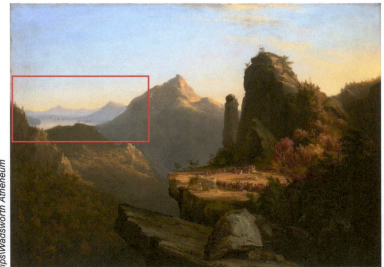

FIGURE 2.24 *Scene from "The Last of the Mohicans,"* (1827), Thomas Cole. Wadsworth Atheneum, Hartford, CT

The color of the sky in the Thomas Cole painting (Figure **2.24**) is blue. The mountains in the foreground are dark brown, but notice how the mountains in the distance are depicted with the color blue. In addition to their small size, the blue color is what makes them appear far away, because they take on the color of the atmosphere, which is light blue.

OPEN VS. CLOSED

Open

Along with several other principles about Renaissance art, Swiss art historian Heinrich Wölfflin (1864–1905) developed the concept of open vs. closed in his *Principles of Art History* (1915). He wrote that paintings and drawings are open when subject matter spills off the edge or is cut off by the picture frame. As viewers, we accept that the figure must have had both legs in the drawing shown here by Michelangelo Buonarroti (Figure **2.25**), but the right leg of the figure is cut off by the edge of the drawing. Similarly, when we take photographs of our friends that frame them so that a face or arm is cut off, the result is an open picture.

FIGURE 2.25 *Drawing for Creation of Adam* (Sistine Chapel, ca. 1508), Michelangelo Buonarroti. Louvre, Paris

FIGURE 2.26 *Madonna of the Meadow* (1505), Raphael Sanzio. Kunhistorisches Museum, Vienna

Closed

Designs are deemed closed when everything necessary to convey the meaning of the image is contained within the picture frame, as in this painting of the *Madonna of the Meadow* by Raphael Sanzio (Figure **2.26**). Things do not conspicuously trail off the edges in most Raphael paintings.

LINEAR VS. PAINTERLY

Linear

Wölfflin also discussed the idea of linear vs. painterly, asserting that paintings are linear whenever hard edges are visible. The *Deposition* by Rogier van der Weyden (Figure **2.27**) is a linear painting even though there are no explicit lines. Hard-edged organic shapes are run up against each other to produce a linear effect such as in the area where the edge of Christ's arm is run up against a black background, and where Mary's blue gown runs up against a green background.

Painterly

Wölfflin said designs are painterly when the edges of objects are blurred or fuzzy. The fuzzy-edged effect results when painters dab their brushes into paint on their palettes and create ragged or blurred edges. Claude Monet's painting of *Gare Sainte Lazare* (Figure **2.28**) is especially painterly, or fuzzy-edged throughout because the painter has dabbed globs of paint onto his canvas without any particular regard for the resulting non-linear quality.

FIGURE 2.27 Detail, *The Descent from the Cross* (ca. 1435), Rogier van der Weyden. Prado, Madrid

FIGURE 2.28 *Arrival of the Normandy Train, Gare Sainte Lazare* (1877) Claude Monet. Art Institute of Chicago, Chicago

SEQUENCE

Sequence is a very special type of repetition in which a continuously changing shape is repeated—usually across an axis. The Alps in the distant background of Leonardo da Vinci's painted landscapes (Figure **2.29**) usually outline the shapes of parabolic arcs (conic sections) that repeat as short sequences.

© National Gallery, London / Art Resource, NY

FIGURE 2.29 Detail, *The Virgin of the Rocks* (1501), Leonardo da Vinci. National Gallery, London

DOMINANCE VS. SUBORDINANCE

Dominance

Dominance, the grandfather of all principles, occurs when one element of art predominates over the others in a design. Pablo Picasso's painting of the *Old Guitarist* shown in Figure **2.30** dominates in the color blue, while Rembrandt van Rijn's *Self-Portrait* shown in Figure **2.31** dominates in the color brown.

Subordinance

A design can dominate in one element or principle of art, but it can also subordinate in another. The Rembrandt painting in Figure **2.33** dominates in the color brown, but some viewers may also perceive a subordinate use of the color yellow or even rusty red.

FIGURE 2.30 *Old Guitarist* (1903), Pablo Picasso. Art Institute of Chicago, Chicago

FIGURE 2.31 *Self-Portrait* (1650), Rembrandt van Rijn. National Gallery of Art, Washington, D.C.

TROMPE L'OEIL (TRICK OF THE EYE)

Trompe l'oeil is a French expression that refers to illusion or double imagery. A bathroom wall can have a window painted onto it, or false architectural features can be painted onto the ceiling of a room; such techniques are very useful in decorating interiors. The architectural frieze shown in Figure **2.32** is painted as *trompe l'oeil* onto a wall to appear three-dimensional, but it is actually a flat painted surface.

FIGURE 2.32 *Trompe l'oeil Frieze on Roman Wall* (ca. 18th century). University of Arkansas, Rome Center

ANALYZING DESIGNS

The technical terms defined above that comprise the elements and principles of art used in many art schools today derive from Western academic instruction rooted in the *Beaux-Arts* (Beautiful Arts) of the French Academy. In addition to these terms, art historians may discuss a painting in terms of its history and/or symbolism—which usually requires additional information to interpret the artwork correctly.

Most visitors to an art gallery today discuss drawings and paintings in terms of a story that the image suggests to them. Much imagination can go into these narratives and this could be one of the important experiences for viewers to art museums. Apart from overtly historical documentaries, however, only a small percentage of paintings have actual stories to accompany them, and those that do usually hearken from the Romantic era (ca. 1800-1850).

ACTIVITY

Let us examine a few paintings first in terms of their narratives and then in terms of their structure as an exercise to employ the technical terms we have discussed. All three Romantic paintings given below are inspired by actual events and seem to cry out for narrative interpretation and explanation.

Fine Art Images/Fine Art Images

FIGURE 2.33 *Raft of the Medusa* (1819), Théodore Géricault. Louvre, Paris

NARRATIVE ANALYSIS

Raft of the Medusa (Figure 2.33)

Based on an actual shipwreck of a ship called the Medusa off the coast of Africa, Théodore Géricault's painting depicts colonists caught up in a storm when traveling to Africa and stranded on the remains of the ship. A man on the upper right waves a flag at the ship that will rescue them. After several weeks adrift on the open sea, only about fifteen survivors survived out of the original one hundred forty-seven passengers; they engaged in the horrific act of cannibalism in order to survive. The painting caused a scandal at the Paris exhibition of 1819 because it depicted so many figures in unflattering nude poses and because it provoked political tensions between liberal and conservative French factions due to its association with the subject of slave trade. The events depicted in the painting take place in a remote location and they project a sense of morbidity, illustrating the alienanne of men from each other.

FIGURE 2.34 *Liberty Leading the People* (1830), Eugène Delacroix. Louvre, Paris

Liberty Leading the People (Figure 2.34)

Based on the Parisian revolution of 1830, Eugène Delacroix's painting illustrates a bourgeois gentleman and peasant boy fighting side-by-side with "Liberty" who is illustrated as a mythical goddess, semi-nude, in Ancient Greek clothing and carrying the French flag. "Liberty" (Marianne) is a symbol representing the French people.

Elements of the French Revolution street riots continued well into the early 19th century in Paris and this painter has effectively given us a scene from that turmoil. Liberty is placed conspicuously at the top of an implied triangle.

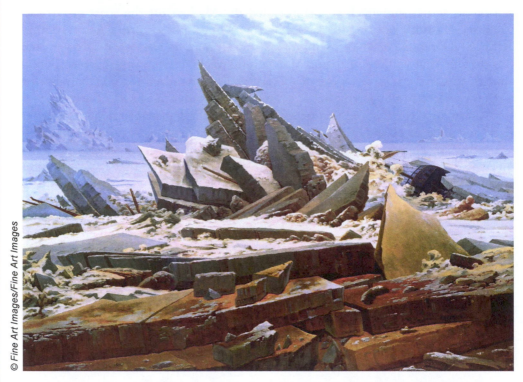

FIGURE 2.35 *Wreck of the Hope* (1824), Caspar David Friedrich. Kunsthalle, Hamburg

Wreck of the Hope (Figure 2.35)

This shipwreck theme illustrates a typical preoccupation of Caspar David Friedrich with death and morbidity. It is based on an actual event—the sinking of a ship on its exploratory journey to the Arctic. Alienation, isolation, and strangeness pervade the scene. Friedrich's paintings usually have one, two, or three people in silhouette looking at the moon or a sunset. In this painting there are no figures at all. A sense of loneliness often prevails in these paintings, and in the *Wreck of the Hope*, one can see the stern of the ship (black shape on the right) as it sinks into the icy waters of the Arctic. The scene is overwhelmed by the presence of the triangular ice pack in the foreground.

STRUCTURAL ANALYSIS

Please write down elements that apply to each painting below. Some elements and principles will apply to only one, and other elements to all three. Please explain how and why your selected elements and principles apply. Compare your list of observations with those of observers given on the following page.

RAFT OF THE MEDUSA Théodore Géricault	LIBERTY LEADING THE PEOPLE Eugène Delacroix	WRECK OF THE HOPE Casper David Friedrich
Fine Art Images/ Fine Art Images	*© Erich Lessing/ Art Resource, NY*	*© Fine Art Images/ Fine Art Images*
ELEMENTS/PRINCIPLES OBSERVED	ELEMENTS/PRINCIPLES OBSERVED	ELEMENTS/PRINCIPLES OBSERVED
-	-	-
-	-	-
-	-	-
-	-	-
-	-	-
-	-	-
-	-	-
-	-	-
-	-	-
-	-	-
-	-	-

Raft of the Medusa (Figure 2.33)

The painting is large and dominates in a brown-ochre color. Staged figures adopt both dramatic and sentimental poses with a lighting that emphasizes *chiaroscuro*. Two large triangles are formed by the stacks of bodies—the "triangle of hope" formed by a pile of people on the right (a man is waving a flag to the ship in the distance that will free them), and the "triangle of despair" formed by the mast and rope surrounding several dead people on the left. The design is replete with organic shapes rendered in a painterly style (blurred edges).

Liberty Leading the People (Figure 2.34)

With reporter-like accuracy of dress, Delacroix painted a predominantly brown-colored landscape with *sfumato* (smoky) effects—gunpowder shots—to represent the fury of the battle. Once again, this is a large painting. Bodies are strewn around the base as in the *Medusa* painting and their flesh is represented with *chiaroscuro*. Note the truncated triangle formed by the French flag at the top; triangles are important motifs in Romantic paintings.

Wreck of the Hope (Figure 2.35)

This is a rather large painting (3' by 5') by Friedrich's standards. Large fragments of ice (triangles and trapezoids) dominate the actual sinking ship (the small dark shape on the right). Friedrich has selected a gray-blue color scheme; the icebergs take on the gray color of the sky as they fade into the distance in this outstanding example of atmospheric perspective. Note the triangular design formed by the fragments of ice in the foreground. There are numerous short sequences (groups of repeated rhomboids) in the ice pack.

HIERATIC ANALYSIS

Unlike the European *Beaux-Arts* that have undergone continual change and improvement, Eastern (Orthodox) Christian art places a high value on preserving tradition (*recension*) or, at least, subjecting any changes to serious critical review. It is safe to say that changes in Orthodox art are seen by the Eastern Church as a form of secularization. Thus, there is a whole tradition of Christian icons that has changed very little across the centuries, and one would better judge these works by using established rules of the church when "reading" them as follows:

1. Centrality—objects in the center are more important than objects on the edge
2. Height—objects at the top are more important than objects at the bottom
3. Relative size—larger objects are more important than smaller ones

In the 14th century Orthodox icon shown in Figure **2.36,** Christ is depicted as he had been for centuries, and as he would be for centuries after —with a beard, a stern look, and dark hair. He is in the center of the icon (1) and positioned in the uppermost area (2) to give him prominence. His image is slightly larger (3) than the surrounding figures, and emphasized with a highlight and *mandorla* (or almond-shaped body halo). In the Eastern Church, these qualities supersede any others that may be present and affect the relative proportion of figures illustrated. What each character or object represents, determines its placement and size.

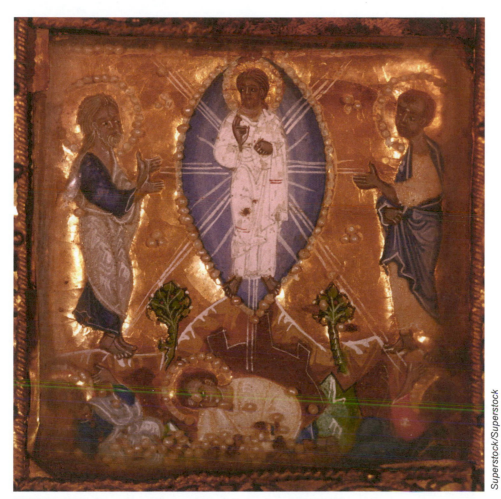

Superstock/Superstock

FIGURE 2.36 *Transfiguration on Mount Tabor* (ca. 1366/1371)

CRITICAL METHOD APPLICATION

Apply the Critical Method to Monet's work, *Arrival of the Normandy Train*. Remember, as discussed in Chapter One, the steps include Description, Analysis, Interpretation, and Evaluation.

FIGURE 2.37 *Arrival of the Normandy Train, Gare Sainte Lazare* (1877) Claude Monet.
Art Institute of Chicago, Chicago

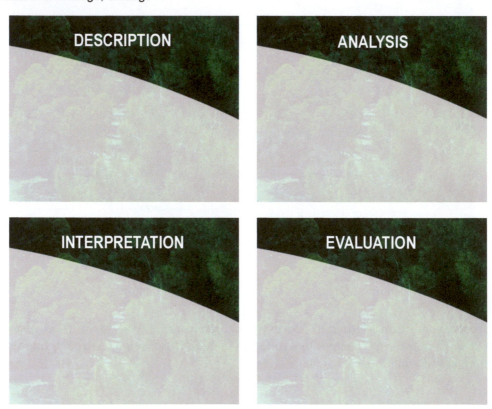

DESCRIPTION

ANALYSIS

INTERPRETATION

EVALUATION

ELEMENTS OF DESIGN

VALUE	Black, white, and all degrees of gray in between
SHAPE	An enclosed area of space
LINE	A connection between two points
TEXTURE	Density of pattern and perceived surface
COLOR	High band frequency in the visual spectrum

PRINCIPLES OF DESIGN

UNITY	Repetition of elements
VARIETY	Contrast in size, shape, density, and color
FOCAL POINT	Point of main interest achieved by value or color
BALANCE	Perceived distribution of visual weight
SCALE/ PROPORTION	Size and quantity of elements within a composition
DIRECTION	A dominant horizontal, vertical, or diagonal trajectory
SPACE/PERSPECTIVE	Representation of space through line, value, or color
OPEN VS. CLOSED	Objects may, or may not be truncated by the picture frame
LINEAR VS. PAINTERLY	Outlines of objects may or may not be blurred
SEQUENCE	Repetition of shapes in ratios to one another
DOMINANCE	One element of art predominates over the others
SUBORDINANCE	A secondary element of the design
TROMPE L'OEIL	Trick of the eye; illusion of reality

HIERATIC DESIGN TERMS

CENTRALITY	Placement in the center is more important than at the edge
HEIGHT	Placement at the top is more important than the bottom
RECENSION	Preservation is good; revision is not
SIZE	Larger objects are more important than smaller ones

ADDITIONAL TERMS

CHIAROSCURO	Contrast between light and dark in rounded objects
CORE SHADOW	Dark shadow located between a highlight and half tone
CROSS-HATCHINGS	Groups of parallel lines that cross at angles

EXPRESSED LINE	A connection between two points
GEOMETRIC SHAPE	Circle, square, triangle, rectangle, oval, trapezoid, etc.
HATCHINGS	Parallel drawn lines
HUE	The name of the color (e.g., blue, red, etc.)
IMPLIED LINE	Juxtaposition of color-valued shapes against one another
ORGANIC SHAPE	Combination of curves and angles that fall into families
SATURATION	The amount of color present
SURFACE TEXTURE	Texture that can be felt with the sense of touch
VISUAL TEXTURE	Texture that results from the subdivision of space

REVIEW QUESTION

Which analytical approach would yield the best results in analyzing the painting shown in Figure **2.38** and why: a structural approach or the hieratic approach?

Christie's Images Ltd./Christie's Images Ltd.

FIGURE 2.38 Chinese ancestor scroll depicting a seated dignitary and his wife with rows of Mongolian men and women (18th century), Anonymous

CRITICAL COMMENTARY

Methods and motives for producing a painting may change, but the universal message of design remains the same. The elements of design are universal across all periods of art history in the West. Knowing critical terms helps one to understand how artists think and how they develop skill at evaluating each other's work.

SCULPTURE

"All art should have a certain mystery and should make demands on the spectator."
—Henry Moore (1998–1986)

INTRODUCTION

Is the image in Figure **3.1** art? Some people give a resounding "no" when asked this question. They recognize the object as a chain intended for something other than art. If you pursue the subject and ask them to explain their responses, they will eventually use terms such as value, shape, line, texture and color—the elements of art—to justify their position. Some will say "It doesn't look like anything to me except an old silver-colored chain" or "The shapes don't mean anything to me." Eventually, however, viewers inevitably resort to the use of critical terms such as shape or color to justify their positions whenever they attempt to evaluate paintings or sculpture. We shall continue to use these terms in this chapter.

Sculpture is found everywhere in our daily lives: in landscape decoration, in cemeteries and public parks, in corporate plazas, and even in family coats of arms. Small examples sit on the shelves of our homes as decorator pieces, or *Tchotchkes*. As consumers, we often express our opinions about sculptors whose work affects us in a deeply personal way—such as dentists and lab technicians who produce three-dimensional crowns for our teeth.

FIGURE 3.1 Unidentified

Like painting, sculpture may be purely decorative and non-representational as in the façades and moldings of a building, or it can be representational as in the great statues of Michelangelo. Sculpture can be examined thematically, placed in a historical context, or interpreted symbolically. Some pieces of sculpture have intrinsic mathematical proportions, while others do not. With such a large range of variables, perhaps the only universal method for discussing sculpture is through the common thread of the elements and principles of sculptural design.

TYPES OF SCULPTURE

FREE-STANDING

The first and most common type of sculpture, free-standing, is found everywhere—indoors within museums and businesses, and outdoors in plazas, parks, and cemeteries. To get the full effect of free-standing sculpture the viewer must be able to move around the object and inspect its articulations as suggested by the object shown in Figure **3.2**. If it is small object such as a votive offering for a temple, one might handle it. If it is a large object such as the *Statue of Liberty*, viewers might be forced to view the behemoth at a distance, or possibly even climb over it. Commercial products often have sculptural qualities because industrial designers have considered the beauty and ergonomic character of the product. Can you think of an object from your daily life that is both free-standing and elegant in design? [Example: desk pencil sharpener]

Robert Alexander/Contributor/Getty Images

FIGURE 3.2 *The Rape of the Sabines.*

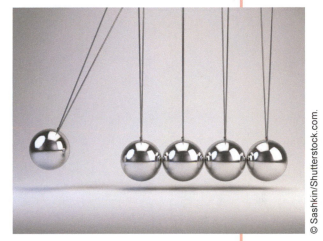

© Sashkin/Shutterstock.com.

FIGURE 3.3 *Newton's Cradle* (background) is an example of kinetic sculpture.

KINETIC

The second type of sculpture consists of objects with moving parts that create animation—or kinetic effects. (Figure **3.3** Newton's Cradle is an example of kinetic sculpture.) Many good examples of this type of sculpture come from George Rickey (1907–2002) who created delicately balanced, wind-activated pieces of sculpture made chiefly from metal parts. Kinetic sculpture fascinates the viewer because of its continuously changing shapes that result from shifting air currents. Can you list an object from your daily life that is an example of kinetic sculpture? [Example: dining room chandelier]

RELIEF

Relief sculpture refers to three-dimensional protrusions relative to a two-dimensional plane. Examples of this technique are found on doorways of churches, temples, and businesses, or in the moldings and trim of ancient buildings. Relief sculpture can occur as low (*bas*) relief where less than half the image protrudes from the surface as in Figure **3.4,** in high (*haut)* relief where more than half of the portrayed image stands out from the surface as in Figure **3.5,** or in sunken relief where images appear below the surface plane as shown in Figure **3.6.** Can you think of an object from your daily life that displays sculptural relief? [Example: kitchen clock]

Source: Steven Husarik

FIGURE 3.4 Bas relief, *Dragon Panel* (1773). Forbidden City, Beijing

Source: Steven Husarik

FIGURE 3.5 Haut Relief, *Façade* (ca. 19th century). Hapsburg Hotel, Vienna

Source: Steven Husarik

FIGURE 3.6 Sunken relief, Detail (ca. 1600–300 B.C.E.). Temple of Amun, Karnak, Egypt

SUBTRACTION/CARVING

The first method consists of carving or removing materials from an existing object. In this technique the artist begins with an object that is larger than the final product and removes all unnecessary material. Michelangelo Buonarroti was probably the greatest subtractive sculptor of all time. You can see his working technique in the *Bound Slaves* (Figure **3.7**) lining the hallway of the Academy of Fine Art (*Accademia di Belle Arti*) in Florence, Italy. He wanted "to free the figure from the stone" and did so by carving away unwanted material from the stone to reveal the human figure. Please give an example of this technique in objects from daily life. [Example: cemetery head stone]

Source: Steven Husarik

FIGURE 3.7 *Bound Slave* (1516–1519), Michelangelo Buonarroti. Academy of Art, Florence

Modern tools such as air hammers and hydraulic wedges make the construction process easier, but *Mount Rushmore* required the same skill at judging proportion and making measurements that early sculptural works required such as Michelangelo's *Bound Slave* shown in Figure **3.7**.

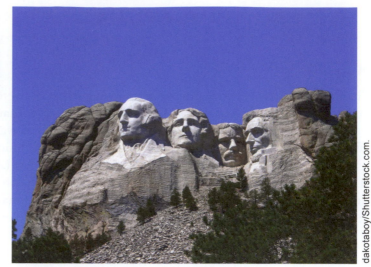

FIGURE 3.8 *Mount Rushmore,* (1927–1941), Gutzon Borglum. Mount Rushmore, South Dakota

ADDITION/ASSEMBLAGE

The addition method consists of combining materials. In this technique the artist builds the work by adding together materials to arrive at a final form. Dale Chihuly creates fascinating pieces of sculpture by mounting glass pieces onto a metal frame (Figure **3.9**). When these works are subjected to a specified indoor lighting the sculptural image is fixed; however, when exposed to daylight, the character of the work can change with the time of day. Please give an example of this technique found in objects from daily life. [Example: wind chimes]

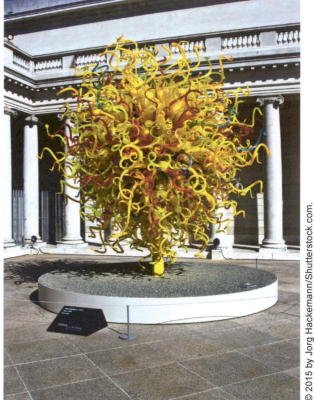

FIGURE 3.9 *Chandelier* (2005), Dale Chihuly. Colorado Springs Fine Arts Center

SUBSTITUTION/CASTING

Another method, substitution, may involve several steps. The bronze *She-wolf* shown in Figure **3.10** was cast using the lost wax process.

A wax model is covered with plaster sections. The plaster sections are broken away from the original, each covered with a layer of wax, and rejoined to create a hollow copy. The copy may then be touched up and improved in terms of its detail. The wax copy is then covered with ceramic slurry and allowed to harden. More slurry is added to the hollowed out portion of the model. After hardening, the entire ensemble is heated, resulting in the loss of melted wax. Molten bronze is poured into the empty space between the inner and outer molds, allowed to cool, and the clay mold segments are removed leaving a positive bronze sculpture.

Sometimes clay is substituted for the wax model, as in the making of bells in the Middle Ages (Figure **3.11**). Wax is placed over this bell-like shape and covered with a slurry or sand mold. Once the ensemble is heated, the wax melts away and the two clay forms are re-joined so that molten metal can be poured into the empty spaces. After cooling, the molds are removed to reveal a bell.

The casting process is used widely for commercial and domestic applications. Some auto parts, for example, are cast with molds. Please give an example of this technique found in objects of daily life. [Example: children's toy soldiers]

FIGURE 3.10 *Bronze She-wolf* (ca. 500 B.C.E. or 800 C.E.). Musei Capitolini, Rome

FIGURE 3.11 *Bell Castings* (2005), Paccard Factory. Annecy-le-Vieux, France

MODELING

Modeling implies the re-shaping or deformation of flexible materials (such as clay or wax). Both Michelangelo and Auguste Rodin sketched many of their statues in clay before they were realized in marble or bronze. This method lends itself to the creation of exotic organic shapes that would be otherwise very difficult to produce by one of the other sculptural methods.

The *Terracotta Warriors* shown in Figures **3.12** and **3.13** were made with two methods—casting and modeling. Although the lower portions of the statues were produced in duplicated sets, the facial features have been shown to be largely individualized from one warrior to another, and sculptors modeled each head using moist clay. Please give an example of modeling of objects in daily life. [Example: ceramic coffee cup]

FIGURE 3.12 *Terracotta Warriors,* (3rd century B.C.E.). Terracotta Warriors Museum, Xian, China

FIGURE 3.13 Detail, *Terracotta Warriors* (3rd century B.C.E.). *Terracotta Warriors* Museum, Xian, China

TEMPORARY INSTALLATIONS

Temporary or conditional art involves transient constructions. The sculptor Cristo and his wife Jeanne-Claude are known to wrap things in fabric—especially large buildings. Christo once wrapped up an entire cliff; about a decade ago he wrapped up three islands near Florida. After wrapping the *Pont Neuf* (New Bridge) in Paris, France, and the *Reichstag* (Parliament building) in Berlin, Germany (Figure **3.14**), Cristo and Jean-Claude ran a length of fabric approximately ten miles across land and down into the Pacific Ocean that was eventually removed. Debates continue about whether or not the films, sketches, and photographs of these temporary constructions are more consequential than the works themselves. Please give an example of this technique found in objects of daily life. [Example: table setting by Martha Stewart for KMart® display]

FIGURE 3.14 *Wrapped Reichstag* (1995), Christo and Jeanne-Claude. Berlin

READYMADES

One of the interesting developments in 20th century art is the use of "readymade" objects to create fine art. A *Coca Cola*® can or *Dr. Pepper*® bottle could qualify as art and might be displayed on a pedestal in a museum if an artist says it is art. Marcel Duchamp went to a factory, picked out a urinal, and put it on display in a New York show in 1917 (Figure **3.15**). Urinals readily bring up associations that conflict with what we ordinarily call museum art and Duchamp's "readymade" caused a stir among visitors to the exhibition. If one considers the shapes of urinals alone, however, they have rather fascinating curves. These days, industrial designers spend much effort in refining both the ergonomics and elegant design of bathroom fixtures—including urinals. Please give an example of this technique found in objects of daily life. [Example: Styrofoam cup]

FIGURE 3.15 *Fountain* (1917/1950), Marcel Duchamp. Philadelphia Museum of Art

ACTIVITY

The objects you selected in the exercises above are examples of industrial design; our lives are intrinsically bound to these objects of commerce. Many talented people enter the field of industrial design to satisfy a desire to gain both the financial rewards and satisfaction of producing attractive designs. Their work is proof that fine art appears around us on a daily basis. Break into groups and develop a short list of five commercial objects from daily life that would surprise us by having attractive sculptural design and locate pictures of these objects online.

ELEMENTS OF DESIGN

The same five elements that apply to flat-pattern design—value, shape, line, texture, and color—apply to sculpture, but with additional elements of space and volume.

VALUE

Please note the range of values in this statue by Antonio Canova (Figure **3.16**). Light and dark patterns are created by the fall of light upon the object—dark organic shapes in the shadows and white organic shapes in the highlights. Can you see the effect of *chiaroscuro* in the legs of the statue?

FIGURE 3.16 *Cupid and Psyche* (1793), Antonio Canova. Louvre, Paris

pseudolongino/Shutterstock.com.

SHAPE

Both positive and negative shapes appear in the sculpture entitled "LOVE" by Robert Indiana. Generally speaking, the objects we identify in a photo are perceived as positive shapes and everything around them is perceived as negative shapes. Can you see the background peering through the holes in the Robert Indiana sculpture shown in Figure **3.17**? If so, you are viewing negative shapes.

Christian Carollo/Shutterstock.com.

FIGURE 3.17 Love (1976), Robert Indiana. Love Square, Philadelphia

LINE

Linear sculpture is achieved by using materials with hard edges that contrast with the background to create implied lines—as shown in Figure **3.18**. Linear qualities can also be achieved by using pieces of wire or neon tubing that serve as explicit lines.

FIGURE 3.18 *Early One Morning* (1962), Sir Anthony Caro. Tate Gallery, London

TEXTURE

The design of this casting from *Trajan's Column* in Rome (Figure **3.19**) is a good example of dense visual texture. Numerous heads of soldiers are combined in sequence with military shields and other paraphernalia to break up the space and increase the density of pattern on this bas relief.

FIGURE 3.19 Detail, "Conquest of Dacia," *Trajan's Column* (113 C.E.). Trajan's Forum, Rome

COLOR

The necklace worn by *Queen Nefertiti* in this bust from Ancient Egypt (Figure **3.20**) was originally made of precious and semi-precious colored stones that are now picked clean. Each stone in the original necklace carefully matched its neighbor in terms of size and character, and must have been strikingly brilliant when new. Color also appears in the paint on the makeup of the face and headdress on this bust. Terms such as hue, saturation, analogous, and complementary colors apply to the world of sculpture just as they do in the world of flat pattern design.

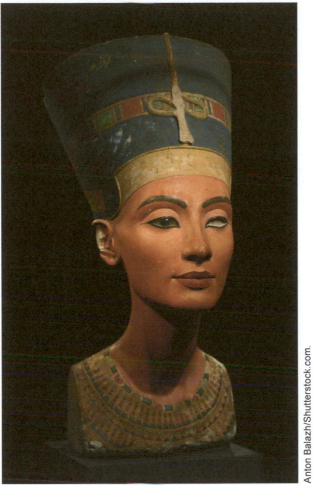

Anton Balazh/Shutterstock.com.

FIGURE 3.20 *Nefertiti* (1345 B.C.E.), Thutmose. Neues Museum, Berlin

SPACE/VOLUME

This additional element of art is applicable here because sculpture exists in space. Sculptors expect viewers to walk around free-standing statuary or to inspect objects from many different angles. Sometimes, pieces of sculpture are so large that viewers must climb over them because of their sheer size—giving them a grand quality.

The message of the *Statue of Liberty* (Figure **3.21**) is lost when it is shrunk down to the size of a souvenir key chain. One of the reasons why we see these artworks in person is to experience for ourselves the effect of space and volume by climbing over them and/or seeing them from different angles.

Ella_K/Shutterstock.com.

FIGURE 3.21 *Statue of Liberty* (1886), Frederic Auguste Bartholdi. New York City

PRINCIPLES OF DESIGN

Works of sculpture employ the same organizational principles as flat-patterned designs.

DOMINANCE VS. SUBORDINANCE

Dominance is an all-governing principle of design in which one element of art predominates over others. A piece of sculpture might dominate in the use of the color red, but subordinate in the color blue. Another piece of sculpture might dominate in the vertical direction, but subordinate in the diagonal direction. The Anish Kapoor sculpture shown in Figure **3.22** dominates in the color blue (reflected color of the sky) and subordinates in gray (value of the reflected sidewalk) because those are the colors of its reflected surroundings.

FIGURE 3.22 *Cloud Gate* (2006), Anish Kapoor. Sculpture Park, Chicago

DIRECTION

Vertical, horizontal or diagonal—there is little doubt about the dominant direction in Constantin Brancusi's sculpture shown in Figure **3.23**.

FIGURE 3.23 *Bird in Space* (1923), Constantin Brancusi. Philadelphia Museum of Art, Philadelphia

PROPORTION

The *Aphrodite of Melos* (*Venus de Milo*) shown in Figure **3.24** has perfect proportion, but not perhaps the kind one might think of immediately. She has mathematically correct proportions. *Aphrodite*, the goddess of beauty, is constructed according to the canons of proportion laid down in the Ancient Greek world. If one were to draw a line from her head to toe, the statue divides in half at the groin area, and at the navel on .62—or the point of the Golden Section. One could continue to divide the statue and find that simple, whole number ratios fall on important anatomical points. Obviously, not all statues from all historical eras have these unique characteristics. Proportion is as much a cultural issue as it is an artistic one.

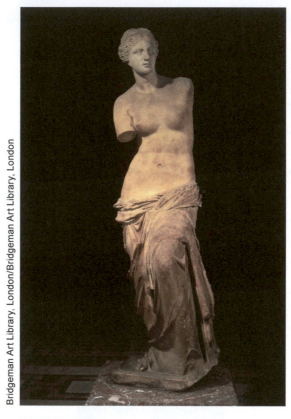

Bridgeman Art Library, London/Bridgeman Art Library, London

FIGURE 3.24 *Aphrodite of Melos, or Venus de Milo*, (Between 130 and 100 B.C.E.). Louvre, Paris

SEQUENCE

Sequence is a repetition of shapes by logarithmic ratios. The *Monument to the Discoveries* sculpture in Portugal (Figure *3.25*) progressively repeats shapes that fan out from its base. Each shape gets progressively larger from the right to the left not simply because of the illusion of receding objects in perspective, but because of increasing size ratios assigned to each shape. Please note that sequence is not simply the repetition of shapes, but a repetition of the same shape growing progressively larger or smaller.

FIGURE 3.26 *Monument to the Discoveries.* Lisbon, Portugal

FOCAL POINT

Robert Smithson's *Spiral Jetty* is hypnotic and the viewer's eye is inevitably drawn to the center of the spiral (Figure **3.26**). Smithson photographed the construction of the work in 1970 (*Spiral Jetty Film Stills*) when the water in the Great Salt Lake was low. When the water table rose years later, however, *Spiral Jetty* disappeared only to resurface again after the lake experienced a drought and the water level receded. Its spiral center is a good example of focal point.

FIGURE 3.26 *Spiral Jetty* (1970), Robert Smithson. Salt Lake City, UT

OPEN VS. CLOSED

The concept of open vs. closed found in Heinrich Wölfflin's *Principles of Art History* is usually applied to paintings, but it can also apply to any relief sculpture defined by a frame.

During the Renaissance, a contest was held to decide who would produce the relief sculpture for large bronze doors on the cathedral baptistery in Florence, Italy. Finalists Filippo Brunelleschi and Lorenzo Ghiberti were asked to illustrate the subject of *The Sacrifice of Isaac* from the Bible. Brunelleschi's losing design (Figure **3.27**) on the left is open (i.e., things trail off the edge of the picture frame at the point of the arrow), whereas Ghiberti's winning design (Figure **3.28**) on the right is closed (i.e., things are contained within the picture frame).

OPEN **CLOSED**

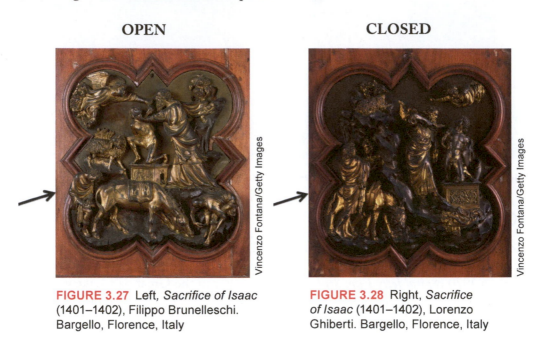

Vincenzo Fontana/Getty Images

Vincenzo Fontana/Getty Images

FIGURE 3.27 Left, *Sacrifice of Isaac* (1401–1402), Filippo Brunelleschi. Bargello, Florence, Italy

FIGURE 3.28 Right, *Sacrifice of Isaac* (1401–1402), Lorenzo Ghiberti. Bargello, Florence, Italy

BALANCE

There are three types of balance: symmetrical, asymmetrical, and radial. If a symmetrical piece of sculpture is cut down its vertical axis, the resulting halves are a mirror image of each other (Figure **3.29**). If the halves are dissimilar, however, the work is asymmetrical, as shown in the work by Isamu Noguchi in Figure **3.30**. Designs with radial balance show equal distribution from a center point as in *The Wheel of Life* from the *Dazu Rock Carvings*, near Chongqing, China (Figure **3.31**). (Please note that the photo is taken from an angle and is circular when seen straight on.)

SYMMETRICAL

FIGURE 3.29 *Entrance Gate.* Versailles Palace (ca.1689–1710), France

ASYMMETRICAL

FIGURE 3.30 *Mantra,* (1966–1985), Isamu Noguchi. Noguchi Museum, Long Island City, NY

RADIAL

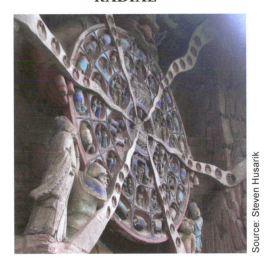

FIGURE 3.31 *Wheel of Life, Dazu Rock Carvings* (9–13th century C.E.). Chongqing, China

UNITY

Unity is created by the repetition and/ or dominance of elements.

GEOMETRIC SHAPES

In Figure **3.32**, the red color and the six flat, square geometrical sides create a very simple and unified piece of sculpture.

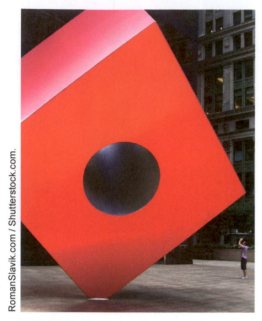

FIGURE 3.32 *Red Cube* (1968), Isamu Noguchi. Noguchi Museum, Long Island City, NY

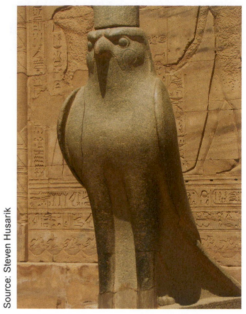

FIGURE 3.33 God Horus, Temple of Horus (ca. 360–343 B.C.E.). Edfu, Upper Egypt

ORGANIC SHAPES

In the hawk-like representation of the *God Horus* (Figure **3.33**) from Edfu, Upper Egypt unity is created by the repetition of a teardrop organic shape throughout the statue in the body, the wings, and even the beak. One might say that the beak of this bird forms the main motif of the statue.

VARIETY

Variety results from many contrasting elements of art, or expanding the number of possibilities within an element. The countless number of organic shapes in the folds of cloth and position of limbs in *Apollo and the Nymphs* by François Girardon (Figure **3.34**) illustrate the principle of variety quite well.

Peter Willi/Peter Willi

FIGURE 3.34 *Apollo and the Nymphs* (1666–1673), François Girardon. Versailles, France

ENVIRONMENT

Whether it is located indoors or outdoors, a sculptor must consider the environment for each work—especially in those intended for outdoor gardens and/ or combined with architecture. The size, approach and effects of weathering were taken into account in *Monument to the Heroic Defenders of Leningrad*. Victory Square. St. Petersburg, Russia (1975), by Mikhail Anikushin (Figure **3.35**).

Peter Barritt / Peter Barritt / SuperStock

FIGURE 3.35 *Monument to the Heroic Defenders of Leningrad* (1975). Mikhail Anikushin. Victory Square. St. Petersburg, Russia

CRITICAL METHOD APPLICATION

Apply the Critical Method to Kapoor's work, *Cloud Gate*. Remember, as discussed in Chapter One, the steps include Description, Analysis, Interpretation, and Evaluation.

FIGURE 3.36 *Cloud Gate* (2006), Anish Kapoor. Sculpture Park, Chicago

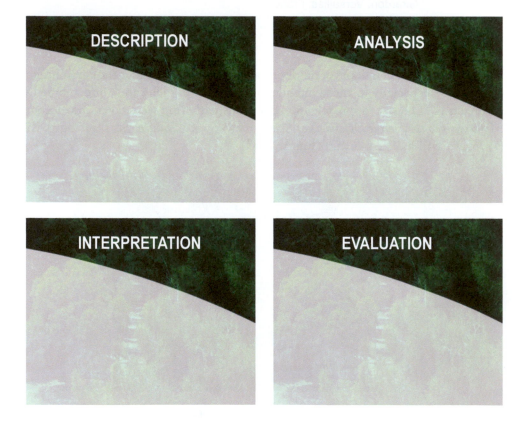

DESCRIPTION

ANALYSIS

INTERPRETATION

EVALUATION

TYPES OF SCULPTURE

FREE-STANDING	Sculpture in the round; often on a pedestal
KINETIC/SUSPENDED	Sculpture with moving parts; often hanging
RELIEF	Three dimensional protrusions relative to a plane

SCULPTURE TECHNIQUES

CARVING	Removing unwanted material
CASTING	Use of molds
COMBINING	Adding together materials
MODELING	Re-shaping plastic materials
TEMPORARY	Installations intended for only a short period
FOUND ART (OBJET TROUVÉ)	Objects from daily life reclaimed as art

ADDITIONAL TERMS

ARTICULATION	Relationship of adjacent shapes
ENVIRONMENT	Lighting and traffic patterns surrounding the art work
ERGONOMIC	Design that maximizes physical utility
MOBILE	Kinetic sculpture that features equilibrium
ENVIRONMENT	Lighting and traffic patterns surrounding the art work

This piece of contemporary sculpture (Figure **3.37**) is a good example of

1. Carving
2. Casting
3. Focal Point
4. Found Art
5. Symmetrical balance. Only one answer applies—all others are incorrect.

(Answer spelled backwards: gnitsac)

FIGURE 3.37 A-maze-ing Laughter (2009), Yue Minjun. Vancouver, B.C.

Josef Hanus/Shutterstock.com.

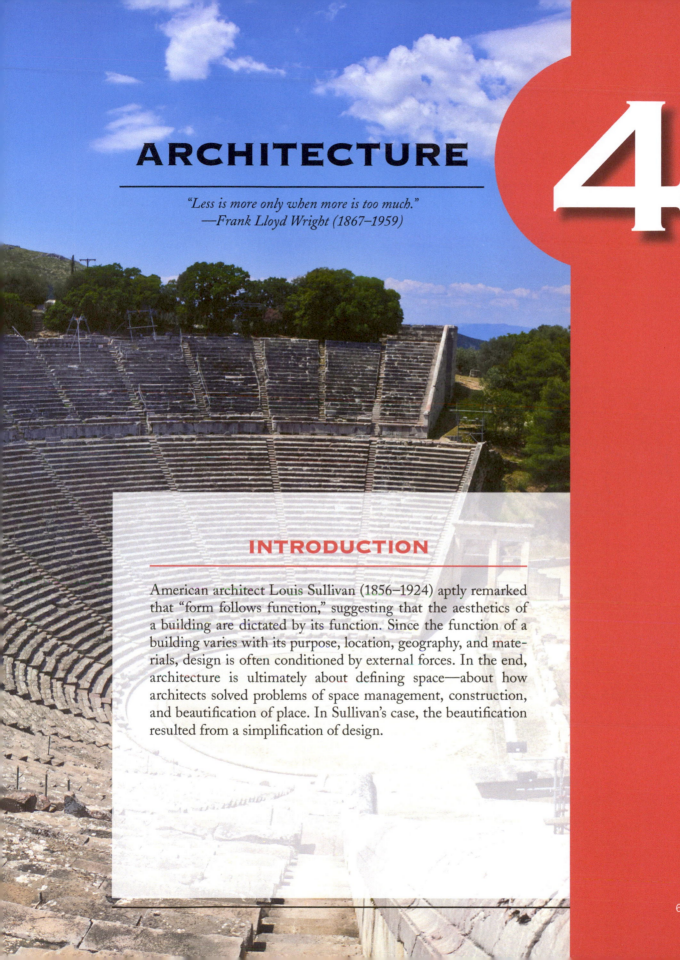

ARCHITECTURE

"Less is more only when more is too much."
—Frank Lloyd Wright (1867–1959)

4

INTRODUCTION

American architect Louis Sullivan (1856–1924) aptly remarked that "form follows function," suggesting that the aesthetics of a building are dictated by its function. Since the function of a building varies with its purpose, location, geography, and materials, design is often conditioned by external forces. In the end, architecture is ultimately about defining space—about how architects solved problems of space management, construction, and beautification of place. In Sullivan's case, the beautification resulted from a simplification of design.

TYPES OF ARCHITECTURE

The types of architecture are 1) residential, 2) industrial/commercial, 3) sacred/religious, 4) government/educational and 5) vernacular/portable.

RESIDENTIAL/DOMESTIC

Architecture of the home was made famous by one of the greatest residential architect in the past century, Frank Lloyd Wright (1867–1959). This chapter includes a discussion of perhaps his most famous residence, *Falling Water*, in Bear Run, Pennsylvania (Figures **4.1** and **4.40**).

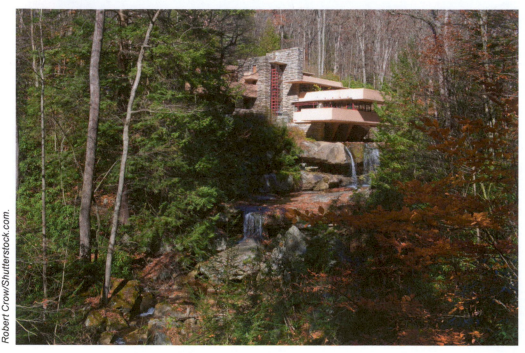

Robert Crow/Shutterstock.com.

FIGURE 4.1 *Falling Water* (1937), Frank Lloyd Wright. Bear Run, Pennsylvania

INDUSTRIAL/COMMERCIAL

Some of the most distinguished and monumental designs in the world fall into the category of commercial architecture; architectural firms vie for opportunities to design office buildings and commercial spaces. Well-known architects and contemporary architectural firms include I. M. Pei (1917–, designer of the entrance to the Louvre), Frank Gehry (1939–, designer of the *Guggenheim Museum* in Bilbao, Spain), the firm of Kohn/Pedersen/Fox (designers of the *World Financial Center* in Shanghai), and Hans Hollein (1934–, designer of *Haas Haus* in Vienna Austria—a notable example of contemporary hotel architecture, shown in Figure **4.2**).

FIGURE 4.2 *Haas Haus.* (2006), Hans Hollein. Vienna, Austria

Source: Steven Husarik

SACRED/RELIGIOUS

Perhaps more than any other genre, the architecture of church, temple, and mosque has displayed both diversity and continuity in style over the centuries. While certain internal demands of a sanctuary govern the approach to and location of sacred altars, new materials have also changed the features of these buildings considerably over the years. Sacred architecture involves the related category of tombs such as the *Giza Pyramids* in Cairo (Figure **4.3**).

FIGURE 4.3 *Sphinx and Khafre Pyramid* (ca. 2570 BC). Giza Plateau, Cairo, Egypt

Source: Steven Husarik

GOVERNMENT/EDUCATIONAL

Before World War II, American government and educational buildings appeared in a variety of architectural styles including Ancient Greek, Roman, and Gothic. After the war, however, architects adopted design concepts that reflected modern abstract definitions of school, office, and institutional architecture. A modern post-war building, the *Marin County Courthouse* (Figure **4.4**) illustrates how unity is achieved by multiplying a single motif—the paper clip shape—throughout the structure. This shape appears in the entry gates, the glass windows of telephone booths, and the horizontal outlines of walkways from one floor to the other.

FIGURE 4.4 a, b. External and Internal Views, *Marin County Courthouse and Civic Center* (commissioned 1955, completed 1960–1969), Frank Lloyd Wright. San Raphael, California

VERNACULAR/PORTABLE

This final category includes some of the most interesting and yet bizarre types of buildings. Hot dog or snow cone stands, stages for rock concerts, and construction toilets all belong to this category. The *Outhouse Society of America*, for example, encourages creativity in the construction of unique vernacular structures. Books have been published illustrating the different types of enclosed latrines—some tall, others square, others oblong, and some with the traditional half-moon over the doorway (Figure **4.5**). Although modern plumbing has made outhouses largely unnecessary, they are suited to a particular time, place, and region and therefore qualify as examples of temporary or vernacular architecture.

ELEMENTS OF ARCHITECTURE

Architecture is similar to sculpture in its incorporation of three-dimensional design— even if the ultimate difference between the two is that the space will be occupied. Thus, the elements and principles of architecture are essentially the same as those for sculpture. When architecture rises above purely practical considerations of

David E. Powers/Shutterstock.com.

FIGURE 4.5 Vernacular Outhouse

engineering, it becomes a form of sculptural design and terms such as unity, line, repetition, balance, scale, and proportion from visual design apply. Several additional items should be added to the list, however, when considering architecture: context, internal space, materials, and climate.

CONTEXT

This term has been mentioned in connection with sculpture (Chapter 2). A sculptor will carefully position a piece of sculpture in an art exhibit in order to maximize traffic patterns around the object and to show off its best side(s). Traffic patterns approaching a building entry are usually designed to maximize the curb appeal, as well. Surrounding landscape features may come into play when positioning a building at a particular site; a building situated on a hill may require special access not necessary in a building sited on flat ground. Additionally, a building may have a political or religious context that influences its physical location.

SPACE/INTERNAL PLANNING

While the approach to a structure is important, the relationship of rooms within and traffic patterns throughout the structure are also important. This is especially true in American homes and businesses where more emphasis typically is placed upon interiors and personal comfort than on the external decorations.

MATERIALS

Since architecture is the study of spatial definition and enclosure, the type of materials used will usually explain the nature of a building. Aluminum and steel affect the type of structure as much as cut stone or mud. Typical modern materials include stone, glass, metal, concrete, wood, fabric, plastic, clay, and recycled brick.

CLIMATE

Climate determines the materials and shape of a building, and even how the building is sited. Adobe construction, suited to the dry climate of Arizona, would not be appropriate for the humid and cold environment of Chicago where the material would fall to pieces. People located in the northern United States need weather resistant and highly insulated buildings because they experience severe winter climates. Solid construction techniques and materials are often modified or omitted altogether in milder southern climates, where structures with un-insulated walls and large windows (unthinkable in northern climates) are the norm.

ACTIVITY

Unless we relate them to our own lives, the elements and principles of architecture may seem boring. However, young married couples know the importance of space planning in remodeling or purchasing a new home; they may haggle over where to put an extra half bathroom, or where the children's rooms will be located, or how the traffic will move to the kitchen from the living room. They may ask themselves "Which wall should be torn down to improve the traffic patterns in this house?" Imagine yourself in a three-bedroom house with two bathrooms, a living room, and kitchen that you want to rehab. You are married and have three children. Draw a circle to represent each room in the house, label each room with the people who will use it. Then, draw lines to connect each circle showing which rooms should be next to each other. The resulting diagram is called an *adjacency diagram* and is used by architects to develop the traffic patterns for homes or businesses.

SIX ARCHITECTURAL TECHNIQUES

Six architectural techniques apply to most styles in the history of Western architecture. Let us briefly review the first two items on the list and then discuss the remaining four in the historical contexts of societies that perfected them.

1. LOAD-BEARING WALL	2. SKELETAL FRAME
3. POST-AND-LINTEL	4. ROMAN ARCH
5. MEDIEVAL ARCH	6. CANTILEVER

LOAD-BEARING WALL BUILDING

All the weight of the building is carried by the walls in a load-bearing wall structure. Thus, the walls must be thick enough for the building to stand. Limitations apply to the achievable height in these load bearing wall buildings since the laws of physics prevent them from exceeding thirteen stories. Carnegie Hall in New York City is an example of a load-bearing wall building (Figure **4.6**). At certain points its lower walls measure approximately twelve feet thick while its upper walls are progressively thinner. Unlike its neighbors, Carnegie Hall is not a skyscraper, nor could it ever become one because of the limitations of load-bearing wall technique.

FIGURE 4.6 *Carnegie Hall* (1890), William Tuthill (1855–1929). New York City

SKELETAL STEEL FRAME STRUCTURES

The buildings surrounding Carnegie Hall, skeletal frame structures, qualify as skyscrapers. In this type of structure, the walls, windows, and doors hang from a steel frame in a skeletal frame structure, allowing it to flex and bend in the wind. Such structures can stand as tall as 100 stories—such as the *Willis Tower* (formerly known as *Sears Tower*) in Chicago or Trump Tower in New York.

The story of skyscraper architecture is essentially the story of American architecture—even though many of the same ideas about skyscraper architecture have traveled across the world to cities such as Kuala Lumpur, Shanghai, Beijing (Figure **4.7**, *CCTV Television Building*), and Hong Kong. Most students are familiar with the appearance of skyscraper and load-bearing wall architecture, so it is more historically and artistically profitable to focus our study upon the four remaining types of architecture: post and lintel, Roman arch, Gothic arch, and cantilever.

FIGURE 4.7 *CCTV Television Building* (2008), Rem Koolhaas (1944–), Ole Scheeren (1971–). Beijing

SELECTED HISTORICAL STYLES

1. Ancient Greek
   Post & Lintel

2. Ancient Roman
   Roman Arch

3. Medieval Gothic
   Arch

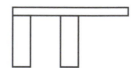

4. 20th Century
   Cantilever

FIGURE 4.8 Four Representative Architectural Motifs

Let us examine the remaining four styles of architecture not only in terms of their applications, but in terms of the societies that brought each to a pinnacle of beauty.

POST AND LINTEL: ANCIENT GREEK

Post and lintel construction is one of the oldest architectural techniques known. In this technique, a lintel (crossbeam or header) passes over top of a void that is supported at either end by posts, pillars, or columns. Stonehenge at Salisbury, England (Figure **4.9**) is an early example of post and lintel structure that illustrates the principle quite well. Stonehenge has been characterized in a number of ways. One of the most interesting interpretations identifies it as a celestial clock for confirming the summer and winter solstice. The machine consists of two concentric circles in post and lintel style that identify the points when the sun rises and sets in various seasons. For those in an agrarian society who wished to keep track of planting and harvesting, a permanent clock like this would have been a valuable tool—an important one to leave to their descendants. The machine was built over many generations of families and remains one of the great monuments to the technological innovation of folk societies.

FIGURE 4.9 *Stonehenge* (ca. 3,000 B.C.E.). Salisbury Plain, England

Stonehenge is an elegant machine whose stones retain much of their natural character even though they follow a prescribed mechanical design. This contrasts sharply with the Ancient Greek attitude about building materials, where almost every aspect of a material (stone) is transformed into a new form. When converting their early wood and mud brick temples into stone, the Greeks treated the stone almost like a bar of soap—carefully shaving away at its contours over centuries to arrive at perfection. This long architectural tradition reached its apex in the 5th century B.C.E. in classical buildings such as the *Hephaisteion* (Temple of *Hephaistos*) in Athens, Greece (Figure **4.10**).

The roots of classical architecture can be traced to a Minoan culture preceding the classical Greek culture located on the island of Crete, about halfway between the Egypt and Greece. A palace at Knossos on Crete was considered a wonder of the world because of its enormous size and complexity. With scores of stairwells and half dozen floors, people at the time saw it as a kind of labyrinth (Figure **4.11**). Inside, a Minotaur who lived there demanded a tribute of young boys and girls each year from the mainland Greeks whom

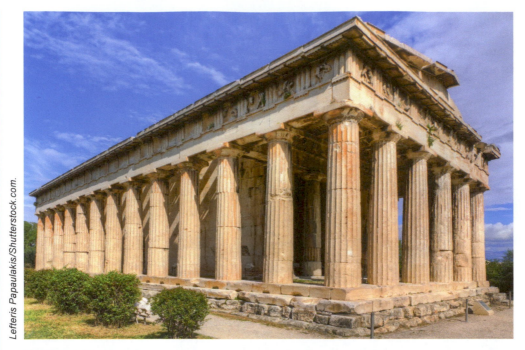

Lefteris Papaulakis/Shutterstock.com.

FIGURE 4.10 *Temple of Hephaestus* (449–414 B.C.E.). Agora, Athens

Lefteris Papaulakis/Shutterstock.com.

FIGURE 4.11 Reconstructed Columns, *Palace at Knossus* (originally constructed ca. 1900 B.C.E.). Crete

they found repugnant. The Athenian Greeks revered Theseus, one of their early Greek kings, because he succeeded in getting into the palace and killing the Minotaur despite the fact that the palace had the appearance of a labyrinth. The columns and capitals of this palace are prototypes for those found later in the classical era.

Half the distance from Knossos to Athens brings one to another important place in Ancient Greek history—the so-called Agamemnon palace at Mycenae (Figure **4.12**) where plans for the Trojan War were laid. Two lions over the entryway represent symbols of power and strength and frame a column shaped like the ones found at Knossos—a narrow shaft at the bottom, wider at the top, and with a capital on top. The residents of this palace apparently wanted the viewer to know that their family roots were traceable to the prestigious palace at Knossos. Ancient Greeks were inclined to preserve their history and refine it, even in purely architectural terms.

Ancient Greek temples from the Classical period (5th century B.C.E., and most of the 4th century B.C.E.) are actually stone copies of wood and mud brick originals. Early Ancient Greek temples were small buildings with pitched roofs and a front porch. Initially, tree trunks may have been used as supports for the extended roof of the porch that were later stylized into columns.

Lefteris Papaulakis/Shutterstock.com.

FIGURE 4.12 "Lion Gate," *Palace of Agamemnon* (ca. 1250 B.C.E.). Mycenae, Greece

FIGURE 4.13 Rear Entrance, *Forbidden City* (ca. 1406–1420). Beijing

PRESERVING THE PAST

The tendency to preserve the past by converting existing structures into new materials is present throughout history. One can easily see it in the evolution of tents into Chinese temples (Figure **4.13**). Originally made of cloth and wooden poles, the tents were converted into wood, stone, and tile to make them resistant to fire. Today, metal poles replace the traditional wooden posts in many restored temples of China.

In the floor plan of an early Greek temple (Figure **4.14**), the front area is called the *pronaos*. Behind the *pronaos* is the *naos*—where the cult statue stood. Keen to preserve every aspect of their history, the Ancient Greeks took the wooden temple and memorialized it in stone—preserving its external appearance and even its various internal parts such as the crossbeams and supports.

NAOS

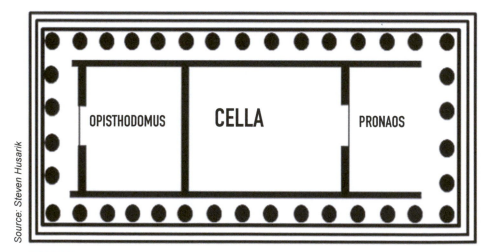

OPISTHODOMUS CELLA PRONAOS

FIGURE 4.14 Floor plan, *Ancient Greek Temple (Hieron)*

In a modern pitched roof garage, the beams that cross the ceiling and carry the weight of the roof also keep the walls from falling apart. In the original Greek temple, those same crossbeams stuck out of the building to form ridges. When these temples were converted into stone, the ridges were retained in the design—even though they were no longer needed for support—and given the name *triglyphs* (Figure **4.15**).

FIGURE 4.15 *Entablature* showing *triglyphs* and *metopes, Parthenon* (447–438 B.C.E.), Ictinus, Callikrates, Phideas. Athens, Greece

Ancient Greeks often filled in the space between the *triglyphs* with pictures or relief carvings called *metopes*—usually portraying scenes from the stories of the gods. *Triglyphs* and *Metopes* are Greek terms for features shown on the *entablature* in Figure **4.15**. The wall elevation of a Greek temple is its order and there are three famous orders of Ancient Greek columns: *Doric, Ionic,* and *Corinthian* (Figure **4.16**). Sometimes a female figure called a *Caryatid* is substituted for the shaft as shown in Figure **4.17** to create a fourth order of columns.

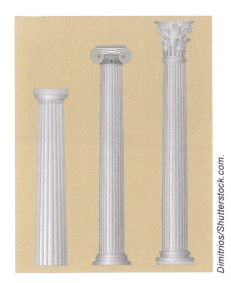

FIGURE 4.16 Ancient Greek Orders of Columns

FIGURE 4.17 "Porch of Caryatids," *Erectheum*, (421–406 B.C.E.), Mnesicles. Acropolis, Athens

Let us read from the bottom to top of these orders. The base is labeled the *stylobate*—a platform on which the building rests and above that sits a shaft or column. Columns are often made of stacked stone cylinders with both male and female ends fitted so precisely that, when viewed from a distance, one cannot tell they are separate pieces of stone. Some shafts have a series of grooves carved across their length called fluting, and they often have a bulge in the middle that is given the name *entasis*. This curved distortion helps the building to avoid looking top heavy.

At the top of the shaft is the capital. The shape of the capital depends upon which order is referenced. A simple disc shape, the oldest, is called the *Doric* order. An unraveled scroll, a later style, is called the *Ionic order*. A clump of *Acanthus* leaves, the latest style, is called the *Corinthian* order. There are variations among the capitals of these basic orders of columns. The capital supports the entablature (lintel) containing either a series of *metopes* and *triglyphs* (in the *Doric* order) or a frieze with continuous sculptural relief (in the *Ionic* order). Above the *entablature* is a large triangular area called the *pediment* (Figure **4.18**) which sometimes houses freestanding statues of gods.

James Becker/Shutterstock.com.

FIGURE 4.18 Façade with Pediment, *Parthenon reconstruction* (1897/1925–1931), William B. Dinsmoor (1886–1973), Russell E. Hart. Nashville, TN

Source: Steven Husarik

FIGURE 4.19 *Maison Carrée* (ca. 16 B.C.E.). Nîmes, France

Recognition of Ancient Greek Style

ACTIVITY

One can find examples in the churches and public buildings today that incorporate the Ancient Greek style. Please identify the orders shown in the examples shown in Figure **4.20** a,b,c.

a. _____

b. _____

c. _____

Source: Steven Husarik

FIGURE 4.20 a, b, and c. Three selected Ancient Greek-style temple orders

Ancient Greek religion was absorbed by Ancient Rome when many of the Greek city-states were turned into "client" states. Roman builders recreated the style of the Greek temple by expanding the stylobate and adding stairs (for public speaking). They also closed off the back of the *peristyle*—as shown in the *Maison Carrée* above. As Christianity spread, cult religions disappeared, leaving both Greek and Roman temples without practitioners. Sometimes Christians converted these temples into churches.

Centuries later, all associations with the original religious practices of these buildings were forgotten and the designs were taken up by Renaissance architects such as Palladio and Brunelleschi.

Subsequent architects adopted the styles for their own use in unrelated buildings such as the *Pantheon (St. Genevieve)* in Paris, France—where Ancient Greek gods of the pediment are replaced with contemporary political figures and attached to a Roman-style building. In Regensburg, Germany, King Ludwig I reconstructed the *Parthenon* and renamed it *Valhalla*, replacing the original Ancient Greek pedimental figures with German gods such as *Wodin, Loki,* etc.

When statesman/diplomat and architect Thomas Jefferson saw the *Maison Carrée* in southern France (Figure **4.19**), he copied the building and was influenced in his designs of the University of Virginia *Rotunda*, and his own home in Monticello. Many American government buildings repeated his designs and the façades of these temples were subsequently incorporated into American churches, libraries, and public buildings. The paint had flecked off by the time Jefferson and other 18th century observers saw the original buildings, and thus they were reproduced as all-white structures.

Find buildings in your region that have Ancient Greek features and then create a new pediment for each building. What figures would you place in the pediment?

ANCIENT ROMAN ARCH/VAULT

Ancient Roman building techniques are based upon the arch. The Romans did not invent the arch nor the method of constructing it, but they used the motif widely in their architecture and brought the building technique to its apex.

Arch building requires a semi-circular wooden frame called a centering (shown in Figure **4.21a**) over which stones are placed continuously until a keystone is inserted at the top. The resulting structure is one of the strongest architectural units known to man because forces applied on the keystone are deflected equally down either side.

Contributed by Colin McClain.
© Kendall Hunt Publishing Company.

FIGURE 4.21 a Roman Arch with centering (forces are distributed equally down each side)

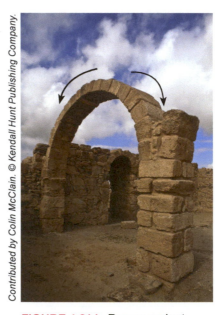

Contributed by Colin McClain. © Kendall Hunt Publishing Company.

FIGURE 4.21 b Roman arch at *Ruins of Roman city Umm Ar-Rasas in North Jordan.* UNESCO World Heritage Site. King's Highway, Jordan, Middle East

One can even construct a Roman arch without mortar by using precisely cut stones, since the force of gravity alone is sufficient to hold the stones in place. However, the Romans usually cemented the stones into place with a concrete mixture made from volcanic ash and lime, called *pozzolan*. After the concrete cures, one can remove the centering and the arch will withstand great stresses.

Repetition and development of the arch as an architectural motif in Ancient Roman architecture is both impressive and imposing. Many Ancient Roman buildings overwhelm the viewer simply by presenting dozens of arches in the form of doorways, windows, and arcades. The arch and its counterparts in the ceiling (vault and dome), allowed Ancient Romans to create vast interior spaces in buildings such as the *Baths of Diocletian*, (Figure **4.25**) or the *Pantheon* (Figure **4.28**).

Arches can be constructed alone or in a series with each other. A row of arches forms a kind of tunnel called a barrel vault (Figure **4.22**). Barrel vaults crossing at right angles are given the name groin vault (Figure **4.23**). Trim applied to the edge of these vaults is called ribbing.

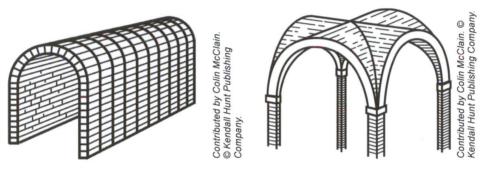

Contributed by Colin McClain. © Kendall Hunt Publishing Company.

Contributed by Colin McClain. © Kendall Hunt Publishing Company.

FIGURE 4.22 Barrel vault (series of arches)

FIGURE 4.23 Groin vault (two barrel vaults crossing at right angles)

Aqueducts—A Series of Arches

Roman society was water driven. Water was needed for both mechanical operations (water wheels) and daily essentials such as water for drinking and bathing. Giant aqueducts, bridges designed to carry water (and in some cases, people and carriages), accommodated the demand for the massive amounts of water that drove the Roman mills and provided drinking water and medicinal water for bathhouses. Note the arcade of Roman arches supporting the aqueduct shown in Figure **4.24**.

FIGURE 4.24 *Pont du Gard* (ca. 1st century C.E.) Nimes, France

Baths—Vaulting

Bathhouses such as the *Baths of Diocletian* (Figure **4.25**) were a combination health club, Rotary club, library, and art gallery all merged into one. People met there for pleasure, health, and to make business contacts. These were enormous buildings with mosaic tile floors and vaulted ceilings. Pieces of sculpture that had been taken from Ancient Greek cities or copied by Greek slaves were on display in the galleries. The buildings required immense ceiling height to accommodate large numbers of patrons.

FIGURE 4.25 *Terme di Diocleziano [Baths of Diocletian]* (298–306 C.E.). Rome

Basilica—Nave and Apse

Another popular building style in Ancient Rome was the basilica or Roman law court. From an architectural perspective, the basilica is defined as a nave (usually with three groin vaults) and an apse. Criss-crossing dotted lines on floor plans of this structure refer to vaulted ceilings. The semi-circular apse was reserved for the seating of a judge (Figure **4.26**).

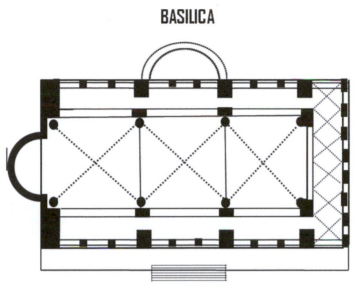

BASILICA

Based on image sourced from Georg Dehio/Gustav von Bezold's Kirchliche Baukunst des Abendlandes. Stuttgart: Verlag der Cotta'schen Buchhandlung 1887–1901, Plate No. 6. Courtesy of Steven Husarik.

FIGURE 4.26 Roman Basilica floor plan

The basilica style is important because it is the architectural model for later Christian churches. When Christianity was proclaimed the state religion of Rome in the 4th century C.E., Christians met in these public basilicas and subsequently built their churches in the same style. One of the earliest Christian basilicas to survive in Trier, Germany (Figure **4.27**) was formerly a law court.

Source: Steven Husarik

FIGURE 4.27 *Basilica of Constantine, or Aula Palatina* (ca. 310 C.E.). Trier, Germany

Pantheon—Drum, Dome, and Greek Temple Façade

The Pantheon is one of the best-preserved buildings from Ancient Rome (Figure **4.28**). "Pan" means all, and "theon" means of the gods, and this is a temple for all of the gods. A very practical people, the Romans brought together all of the gods of the Empire into one conveniently located temple in downtown Rome.

Although it has a post and lintel Greek façade, the *Pantheon* is constructed as a drum with a dome (a dome is defined here as an arch rotated 360 degrees). Renaissance architects such as Bramante, Brunelleschi, and Palladio picked up the idea of placing a Greek temple façade onto a building with a dome and the style of the Pantheon was repeated in other buildings throughout history. Government buildings, museums, and even small churches throughout the United States mimic this style of architecture.

Renata Sedmakova/Shutterstock.com.

FIGURE 4.28 *Pantheon* (rebuilt 126 C.E.). Rome

Colosseum—Amphitheater

A famous stadium from Ancient Rome known as the *Flavian Colosseum* is actually a colossal amphitheater—or two half (Greek) theaters joined together (Figure **4.29**). The *Flavian Colosseum* was built over a bog and plumbing with valves that made it possible to flood the arena for naval battles. The outside of the *Colosseum* was decorated with the historical order of columns from the bottom to the top: *Doric* on the bottom, *Ionic* next, and *Corinthian* next. A Roman invention, the *pilaster* (a half-carved square column in a wall), completed the series at the top.

FIGURE 4.29 *Colosseum*, or *Flavian Amphitheater* (70–80 C.E.), Rome

MEDIEVAL ARCH

There are well over 100 medieval cathedrals around Europe (Figure **4.30**). Some were built in as little as twenty years, while some took seventy-five or more years to finish. Because of their visual complexity and repetitive patterns, the construction methods of

FIGURE 4.30 Façade, *Notre-Dame de Reims* (ca. 1211–1275 C.E.). Reims, France

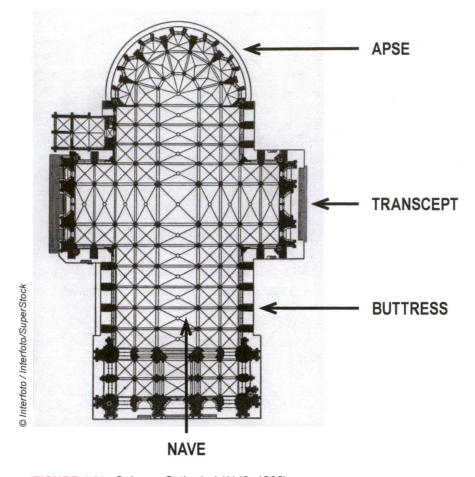

APSE

TRANSCEPT

BUTTRESS

NAVE

© Interfoto / Interfoto/SuperStock

FIGURE 4.31 Cologne Cathedral (1148–1880)

cathedrals are not readily apparent. Therefore, it is helpful to build one from the ground up in order to understand the structure. Let us begin with the floor plan (Figure **4.31**).

Cathedrals are based upon the Roman basilica style with three adjacent aisles—a main aisle called a nave and two side aisles. Nave is the root word of naval, meaning ship; the nave is the ship that carries the worshiper forward toward the altar. The crossing—called a transept—is often positioned on the nave to form a Latin cross.

Several spiral staircases (shown as circles) lead downstairs to a crypt or upstairs to the vaulting (ceiling). Internal vaulting is shown as dotted lines on this floor plan. The floor plan only partially explains the inside and outside of a cathedral. In order to further clarify the structure, one needs to begin at the bottom of the building and extrude it from the base up to the roof.

First, the ground is excavated and footings are put in place to support giant piers. Piers look like columns because they are topped with capitals; however, piers are constructed out of bricks and mortar and supported by excavations sunk into the ground. This contrasts with columns that are solid stone cylinders (originally stacked cylinders) on a surface base (*stylobate).*

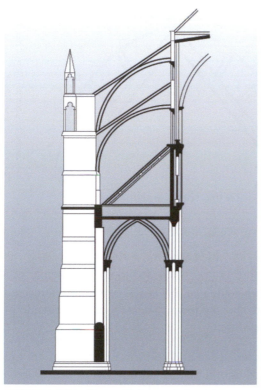

FIGURE 4.33 External view of flying buttresses, *Notre-Dame de Reims* (1211–1275 C.E.). Reims, France

FIGURE 4.32 Cross section, Flying Buttresses

The roof of a cathedral cannot sit upon piers alone because its weight would deflect them outward. In order to manage these forces, so-called flying buttresses redirect the forces of the roof to thick buttress walls shown on the left side of the diagram in Figure **4.32**. Buttresses and flying buttresses form a very complex visual pattern on the exterior surfaces of medieval cathedral (Figure **4.33**) and explain why first-time viewers see cathedrals as somewhat confusing. Once the main piers and buttress walls are in place, the triangular-shaped roof is placed on top.

There are two rows of flying buttresses. One row of flying buttresses supports the roof of the cathedral, while another row supports the ceiling (vaulting) beneath the roof. A special circular ladder is needed to lift large centerings to the top of the building so that the vaulting can be installed (vaulting is a ceiling), and this device is called the Great Wheel (Figure **4.34**). When a man walks inside the Great Wheel, a rope winds up around it to form a giant winch that lifts the centerings into place at the top of the cathedral.

Once the centerings are in place, they are covered with stone blocks to form Gothic arches (Figure **4.35**) and are locked into place with keystones. The process is repeated across the ceiling until the vaulting is complete. Like the roof, the forces of the vaulting are directed down into the buttress wall via flying buttresses.

FIGURE 4.34 Great Wheel

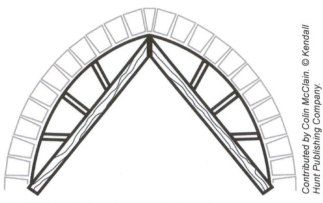

FIGURE 4.35 Gothic shape derived from two *centerings*

In effect, there are two separate ceilings in a Gothic cathedral—the vaulting, and the roof. For this reason, the interior of the building (Figure **4.36**) looks completely different from the outside (Figure **4.37**) and this adds to the visual confusion perceived by the first-time viewer. Everything points sharply toward heaven on the outside of the building, while the interior space is curvilinear.

The Gothic arch brought a new sense of open space and community to architecture. Pointed arch windows allowed much more light into the edifice than earlier semicircular Roman style churches. The stone vaulting also has the practical value of fireproofing the building. If lightning strikes, only the roof will burn and fire will not be able to drop into the building.

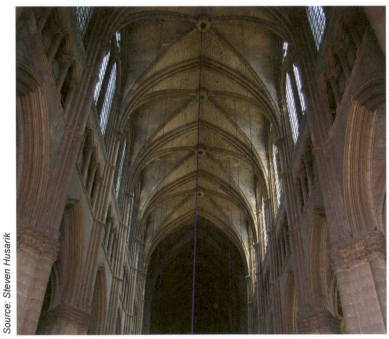

FIGURE 4.36 Vaulting, *Notre-Dame de Reims* (1211–1275 C.E.). Reims, France

FIGURE 4.37 *Notre-Dame d'Amiens Cathedral* (1220–1270 C.E.). Amiens, France

FIGURE 4.38 Doorjambs (in sets of nine), *Notre-Dame d'Amiens*. Amiens, France

Cathedrals are visual sermons about Christianity that contain historical symbolism—including pieces of sculpture that depict Christ, the saints, and other famous biblical heroes. Various design features such as the rose window (the rose is the symbol of Mary, the Mother of Christ) add to the symbolism. Cathedral floor plans and walls are often laid out in holy numbers of 3, 4, 7, 9, and 10. There are three main aisles (Father, Son, and Holy Spirit), and doorjambs are often designed in sets of four (Matthew, Mark, Luke, John), seven (Seven Deadly Sins), or nine (a multiple of three) as shown in Figure **4.38**. Visual repetition with holy numbers is a central feature of medieval cathedral design.

MODERN CANTILEVER

In architecture, the cantilever principle is essentially a teeter-totter that is attached at one end. The vertical support in the middle (post) serves as a fulcrum, and the teeter-totter beam functions as the lintel (Figure **4.39a**). If one applies a force on one end of the teeter-totter, the other end will go up unless securely attached or matched by an equivalent counter force. The weight delivered, the strength of the crossbeam, and the strength of the attachment all contribute to the success of this structure. The teeter-totter can extend out over a hill as shown in Figure **4.39a**.

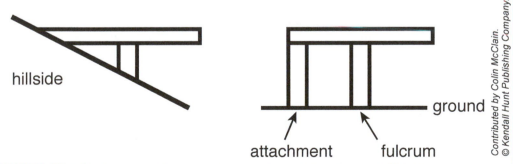

hillside

ground

attachment   fulcrum

FIGURE 4.39 a, b. Principle of Cantilever illustrated on a flat surface and hillside

ARCHITECTURE

Frank Lloyd Wright's *Falling Water* (Figure **4.40**) is a good example of the latter technique. Located on a piece of property owned by Pittsburgh businessperson Edgar J. Kaufmann, slabs of concrete are canted out over an existing waterfall to create a perfect amalgamation of architecture and nature. Kaurfmann visited this area on weekends to get away from the hustle and bustle of the city. He liked to sit on his favorite rock and listen to the sound of the water splashing down into the gorge and decided to commission this house. Wright's solution looks as modern today as it did seventy-five years ago and stands as one of the great achievements of modern domestic architecture and also the principle of cantilever. Amazingly, Wright drew the plan for this home in just one sitting while his student architects looked on at his school in Taliesin, Wisconsin.

Frank Lloyd Wright is credited with initiating the concepts of organic architecture (a home should be suited to the environment in which it is situated) and open planning (air should circulate freely above and throughout rooms). The concept of open planning is used widely in telemarketing businesses today—where employees sit in small cubicles with the air of the HVAC flowing freely above them.

There are many interesting offshoots of cantilever structure in modern architecture. The *Marina City* twin towers located in Chicago use a concrete core as the fulcrum and rooms are balanced out from all sides (Figure **4.41**).

FIGURE 4.40 *Falling Water* (1935), Frank Lloyd Wright. Bear Run, Pennsylvania

FIGURE 4.41 *Marina City* (1964), Bertrand Goldberg. Chicago

CRITICAL METHOD APPLICATION

Apply the Critical Method to Wright's work, *"Falling Water."* Remember, as discussed in Chapter One, the steps include Description, Analysis, Interpretation, and Evaluation.

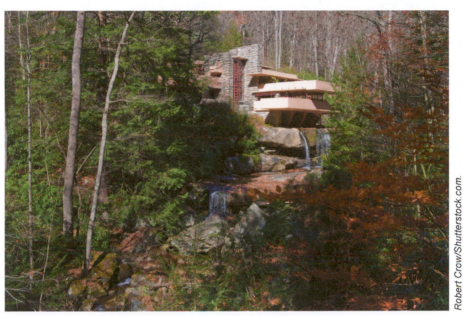

FIGURE 4.42 *Falling Water* (1935), Frank Lloyd Wright. Bear Run, Pennsylvania

Robert Crow/Shutterstock.com.

DESCRIPTION

ANALYSIS

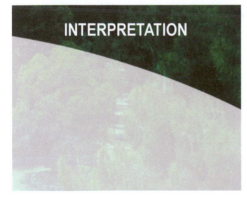

INTERPRETATION

EVALUATION

TYPES OF ARCHITECTURE

RESIDENTIAL	Architecture of the home
INDUSTRIAL	Architecture of business
SACRED	Architecture of church, synagogue, or temple
GOVERNMENT/ EDUCATIONAL	Architecture of the school, offices, institutions
VERNACULAR/ PORTABLE	Architecture suited to a particular time, place or setting

ELEMENTS OF ARCHITECTURE

UNITY	Repetition of motifs or structures
BALANCE	Physical and visual weight on the sides of the structure
SCALE/PROPORTION	Relation of shapes within and around the structure
CONTEXT	Building is suited to the physical, political, or religious location it will occupy
SPACE	Traffic patterns and adjacencies are organized within the structure
CLIMATE	Determines the materials and type of structure

SIX STRUCTURAL TECHNIQUES

LOAD BEARING	Weight of the building is carried by the walls.
SKELETAL FRAME	Weight of the building is carried by a flexible steel cage
POST AND LINTEL	Weight of the building is carried by the posts
ROMAN ARCH	Weight of the building is deflected through semi-circular keystone arches
GOTHIC ARCH	Weight of the building is deflected through angled keystone arches
CANTILEVER	Weight of the building is carried by a fulcrum and counterbalance

ADDITIONAL TERMS

Ancient Greek

CAPITAL	Uppermost member of a column carrying the weight of the entablature
CARYATID	Sculpted human figure replaces a column
CELLA	Entire central region of an Ancient Greek temple

CORINTHIAN	Shaft is capped with acanthus leaves
DORIC	Shaft is capped with a cushion-shaped capital
FLUTING	Longitudinal grooves on a shaft
IONIC	Shaft is capped with an unraveled scroll
METOPE	Spaces between *triglyphs*, sometimes with relief carvings
NAOS	Location of the cult statue in an Ancient Greek temple
PEDIMENT	Triangular area sometimes containing statues of the Gods
POST AND LINTEL	A beam (lintel) that is supported by posts
POZZOLAN	Volcanic ash and lime used as a form of cement
PRONAOS	Entry space to an Ancient Greek temple
SHAFT	Column between capital and base; stacked stone cylinders
STYLOBATE	Top platform in the base of a Greek temple
TRIGLYPH	Three ridges reminiscent of cross beams

Ancient Roman

APSE 1	Semi-circular area for seating of judge in basilica
APSE 2	Semi-circular area for placement of altar in basilica
AQUEDUCT	Bridge or tunnel for carrying water
ARCH	Inverted semi-circular shape made typically of masonry
BASILICA 1	Roman law court
BASILICA 2	Nave and apse
BARREL VAULT	Series of arches
CENTERING	Wooden support used to construct an arch
CIRCUS	Arena for chariot races
COLOSSEUM	Arena for gladiatorial events
DOME	Arch rotated 360 degrees
GROIN VAULT	Two barrel vaults crossing at right angles
VAULT	Ceiling made from semi-circular centerings

Medieval

APSE	Semi-circular area for placement of altar
FLYING BUTTRESS	Masonry support that deflects weight from ceiling or roof
GREAT WHEEL	Large winch used to haul equipment to roof of cathedral
NAVE	Main aisle in a cathedral that leads to the altar
PIER	An upright support akin to a column
TRANSEPT	Crossing of a church or cathedral
VAULT	Ceiling made from pairs of centerings

Modern

CANTILEVER	Fixed teeter-totter
OPEN PLANNING	Upper portions of interior walls are removed to allow free flow of air
ORGANIC ARCHITECTURE	Building should be suited to the site for which it is intended

REVIEW QUESTION

The following illustration (Figure **4.43**) is a good example of:

1. Post and Lintel
2. Roman Arch
3. Gothic Arch
4. Skeletal Frame

Answer spelled backwards: letnil dna tsop

Source: Steven Husarik

FIGURE 4.43 *Breedlove Building* (1976). University of Arkansas – Fort Smith

CRITICAL COMMENTARY

Architecture does not exist in a vacuum. Christian cathedrals evolved from Roman basilicas and large American sporting arenas owe their origins to similar buildings from Ancient Rome. The study of architectural history sharpens the critical senses—making us aware of long-standing architectural solutions that continue to work today. As well, architectural styles illustrate how culture has evolved socially. The Romans, for example, used the arch to create large interior spaces that enabled people to congregate safely out of the weather in large numbers. Cultural history was changed thereafter as public spaces became increasingly important.

MUSIC

"My ideas become tones that resonate, roar, and rage until the conception rises up before me."
—Ludwig van Beethoven (1770–1827)

INTRODUCTION

Because there are so many styles and types of music and so many analytical variables, perhaps the only universal method for discussing music is through the common thread of the elements of music. Knowing these critical terms is the first step toward understanding music from any of the basic traditional style periods known as Baroque, Classic, Romantic, and Modern.

Listen to the following excerpt (Figure **5.1**) and decide whether it qualifies as a piece of music. Please give reasons to justify your conclusions.

Source: Steven Husarik

FIGURE 5.1 Piano Keyboard

 **UNKNOWN EXAMPLE**

Suggestion for additional listening that may be a challenge to assess:

Ketjak, Balinesian Monkey Chant, from the Island of Bali in the Indonesia Peninsula.

Music from the Morning of the World, Nonesuch H72028

Responses

YES, IT'S MUSIC	NO, IT'S NOT MUSIC
IT HAS UNUSUAL **TIMBRE**	IT'S RANDOM
IT HAS **DYNAMICS**	IT IS JUST REPETITIOUS NOISE
IT'S CATCHY	IT HAS NO **HARMONY**
IT HAS A NEW SOUND	IT HAS NO **RHYTHM**
IT HAS **TEXTURE**	IT HAS NO **MELODY**

It does not really matter whether or not you think the unknown example is music, since it is given here simply to evoke responses. If pressed, listeners invariably use technical terms to defend their positions on whether or not something they hear is music. At first, they may say, "it's catchy," "It's got a beat," or "It sounds like chaos." If one pursues the subject with them further, they will eventually use words such as rhythm, melody, and dynamics—the elements of music—to justify their conclusions.

Musicians also use these critical terms to describe music. Like doctors in an operating room who have their own professional vocabulary (e.g., *proximal*, *distal*, *suture*, etc.), musicians have developed an extensive vocabulary unique to the field. The field of music largely responsible for the preservation and history of emerging musical terminology is called musicology—divided into the areas of music theory and music history.

ELEMENTS OF MUSIC

Musicians do not agree on the exact number of elements in music. Some say six, some say seven, and some say that there are just three elements of music. Let us explore the most common terms and their generally accepted definitions. Short excerpts (5–15 seconds each) have been prepared for each of the examples presented in this chapter by composer Darren Rainey. These examples are available online and should be played in a separate window on your computer while you read the text below. They are available in both PC and MAC formats. Please note that most of the supplementary examples mentioned in this discussion are available on NAXOS and/or YouTube.

poztos, 2013/Shutterstock.com.

FIGURE 5.2 Andras Barlay accompanied by Balint Balashazy, Pesterzsebet Art Gallery (2009). Budapest, Hungary

MELODY

 1. 2.

A melody is a rhythmically organized collection of pitches—usually heard prominently above any background notes. The singer in Figure **5.2** would be clearly audible above the accompaniment of the piano.

ACTIVITY

Compare Examples 1 and 2 in MELODY and determine which of the two sounds like a melody to you.

Most listeners feel that Example 2 is more like a melody. That example sounds more like a melody to them probably because it has the following repeated pattern of longs and shorts:

PATTERN:	Long/ long/ short/ long/	long/ long/ short, short

Rhythmic repetition is one factor that determines melodic organization, but there are other equally important factors that contribute to the perception of a group of notes as a melody. Its contour must be smooth enough that one is able to sing it, and it must have unique characteristics that make it memorable.

Suggestions for Additional Listening:

Schoenberg's *Piano Suite* Opus 25 contains melodic ideas that are very difficult to sing.

"Memory," from *Cats*, by Andrew Lloyd Weber is very singable and memorable.

3. CONJUNCT CONTOUR

Some melodies are consistently conjunct—that is they rise, fall, or hover around only a few notes using stepwise motion and this makes them much more easily sung. The example here is limited to just a few notes. It rises through a few notes and then descends a few notes, or repeats the same note again.

Suggestions for Additional Listening:

Any "Kyrie," from plainchant sung by Christian monks

"The Rose," by Bette Midler

4. DISJUNCT CONTOUR

Other melodies are disjunct, and jump around the pitch spectrum. There are many leaps and skips in the Example 4 melody. Sometimes the high and low points of a melody are organized to give it a sense of progress.

Suggestions for Additional Listening:

"Alberich's aria," at the beginning of *Das Rheingold*, in Der Ring

 ## 5. SYLLABIC

(http://en.wikipedia.org/wiki/Dies_Irae#Musical_settings **please scroll to bottom**)

Melodies are said to be syllabic when they have only one note per syllable of text. Christian monks who sing the "Dies Irae" or "Day of Wrath" from the traditional church service (Mass for the Dead) usually sing syllabically in order to emphasize the meaning of the words. The text warns: "Day of Wrath, Day of Mourning!" Since this is an admonition, the singers want to emphasize the text by placing every syllable of the text on a single note.

LATIN	ENGLISH
Dies Irae! Dies illa!	Day of wrath, Day of mourning, that day
Solvet saeculum in favilla	Will dissolve the world in ashes
Teste David cum Sibylla	As foretold by David and the Sybil

6. MELISMATIC

The clarinet-like sound in this example is ornamented with many pitches. When such melodies are coupled with speech, and each syllable of a word has many pitches assigned to it, the melodies are said to be melismatic.

Suggestions for Additional Listening:

Southern gospel music

Whitney Houston singing

ACTIVITY

1. Sing "Row, row, row your boat" together in unison.
2. Sing "Row, row, row your boat" with delayed entrances—camp song style.

You are now hearing both polyphony (separate melodies) and harmony (simultaneous notes).

HARMONY/CHORDS

 1. In a nutshell, harmony is the organization of chords according to dissonance and consonance. A chord is three or more notes played at the same time.

WHEN YOU HIT YOUR FIST ON THE KEYS OF THE PIANO, THAT'S A CHORD

It is a very dissonant chord called a chord cluster. Chords come in more refined varieties than simply fistfuls. Special types of three-note chords, called "triads," are much more consonant than a fistful of notes. Even among the triads, however, there are gradations and levels of dissonance. Members of the chamber ensemble shown in Figure **5.3** are creating harmony by performing groups of simultaneous notes (chords) one after the other.

Igor Bulgarin/Shutterstock.com.

FIGURE 5.3 Members of the QUINTA Orchestra performing music of John Williams, December 19, 2011. Dnepropetrovsk, Ukraine

Consonant and Dissonant Triads

There are two different kinds of triads, consonant and dissonant; musical action is propelled forward by alternating them. The ear likes to hear consonant triads, but tires of them in perhaps in the short space of a second or two. In order to keep the listener's attention, a composer may quickly switch to a dissonant triad—which is harsh to the ear. The ear rejects this noisy triad and wants to return to a consonant one, but things get boring rather quickly on a consonant triad, and so the composer moves again to another dissonant one.

Typical Musical Flow

CHORD: DISSONANT---CONSONANT--DISSONANT----CONSONANT---etc.

Dissonant and consonant alternation of chords propels the music forward just like *peristaltic* waves move food forward through the human gut. It is not even necessary to have a beat in music to achieve the sensation of forward motion in time when chords alternate in this manner. The rate at which composers change chords is called *harmonic rhythm*.

During communion at some churches, the organ plays very softly—with no noticeable beat, yet the music seems to go forward. What propels it forward is the slow, but continuous shift from consonant to dissonant chords. One hears the same effect in old TV soap operas from the 1950s, where a Hammond organ softly plays chords without a beat. The action moves forward because the chords are slowly changing back and forth from consonant to dissonant.

 ## 2. CHORD CADENCES

Some of the most famous groups of chords are called cadences—and they occur at the ends of sections of music. When you hear the famous "full authentic cadence" given in the audio Example 2 you will immediately recognize it.

These chord patterns are so common they bore the average listener today. It would be unheard of for a piece of Rock music, for example, to end with one of these chord cadences. Many pieces of Rock music fade out at the end just to avoid them—even though the chord cadences may form the basis of what is heard throughout the body of the work.

 ## 3. MAJOR   ## 4. MINOR

One of the basic distinctions in harmony is between happy (major) and sad (minor) music.

Does audio Example 3 sound like a happy (major) piece to you?

Suggestions for Additional Listening:

Eine Kleine Nachtmusik (Serenade No. 13 for strings in G major), K.525 by Mozart

"Happy Girl" from *Aquarium* by Aqua

Does audio Example 4 sound like a sad (minor) piece to you?

Suggestion for Additional Listening:

The opening movement of the "Pathetique" *Piano Sonata* by Beethoven

We have strong associations with these major (happy) and minor (sad) sounds in music. Some of our perceptions are linked to training and others are found in the nature of how chords are constructed.

FIGURE 5.4 Queen's Guards, "Changing of the Guards." Buckingham Palace, London

RHYTHM

 **1. PULSE   2. NON-PULSE**

Rhythm is the organization of musical events in time using beats, or pulses. Some religious music of the past does not use pulse beats, but dance music and other forms of entertainment cannot exist without it. Gregorian chant is a good example of music without a pulse beat, while rock music cannot exist without it.

Suggestions for Additional Listening:

Any Gregorian chant

Virtually any rock or jazz music

 **3. FAST TEMPO**

Pulse beats drive the music forward. Sometimes pulse beats are fast, as in a quick-time march…

Suggestion for Additional Listening:

Any quick-time Souza march

 **4. SLOW TEMPO**

Sometimes pulse beats are slow, as in a funeral march.

Suggestion for Additional Listening:

"*Marche Funèbre: Lento*," Movement No. 3, from *Piano Sonata* No. 2, F. Chopin

"*Marche Funèbre: Adagio assai*," Movement No. 2, from *Symphony No. 7*, L.van Beethoven

♪ 5. RUBATO

In most musical compositions the pulse beat is steady, but in some music the beat speeds up and slows down according to what is called *rubato*. If you use a metronome (a device that produces clock-like steady beats), you will hear that the pulse beat in the next example speeds up and slows down (i.e., a steady metronome or ticking clock cannot match the beat). If you are good at tapping out a steady beat you'll notice that your hand has to speed up and slow down to stay with the pulse beats in this recording.

Suggestion for Additional Listening:

Any Chopin piano piece

In order to achieve fast notes in Western music, composers subdivide long notes (generally the pulse beat) into sets of two or three short notes. If faster notes are desired, the composer subdivides the short notes again into shorter twos or threes as shown in the diagram:

Pulse beat	O	long notes
	/ \	
subdivision 1	O O	short notes
	/ \ / \	
subdivision 2	O O O O	very short notes

Thus, the fast notes of our music are subdivided from the slowest. Composers typically like to subdivide slow notes into fast ones to create a dense texture. This is comparable to the way we subdivide our computer programs into "trees."

ACTIVITY

1. One group should pound their fists slowly on a table.
2. Another group must hiss on notes twice as fast as the fists.
3. Another group should clap hands every second and fourth beat.

Once the complete ensemble plays, you can hear rhythm subdividing, rhythm in syncopation, and timbral differences between the notes.

FIGURE 5.5 Pipe organ. St. Gertruda's Church, Riga, Latvia. J.D. Felsko (1866)

DYNAMICS

1. Dynamics refers to the loudness and softness of sounds and all degrees in between. The pipe organ shown in Example **5.5** is capable of both soft and loud sounds, as well as multiple dynamic levels at any particular moment. When many dynamic levels are present in a piece of music, the phenomenon is labeled *polydynamics*.

Suggestion for Additional Listening:

Almost any piano piece

2. TERRACE DYNAMICS

Sometimes several dynamic levels, or terrace dynamics, are due to the number of players performing. Mixing various group sizes results in terrace-like steps of loudness. The more players that play, the louder the music sounds. This musical effect is present in all periods of music, but especially in Renaissance and Baroque music. (Do you notice how this audio example switches back and forth between a small and large ensemble?)

Suggestions for Additional Listening:

"Brandenburg" *Concerto No. 1*. J. S. Bach

"In America," *Full Moon Album*. Charlie Daniels Band

3. DYNAMIC CURVE

Sometimes changes of dynamic level are due to a progressive increase in loudness called *crescendo*, or decrease in volume called *decrescendo*. When such changes from soft to loud occur over an extended period of time, they are referred to as dynamic curves. Romantic music predominates in the use of dynamic curves.

Suggestion for Additional Listening:

Arabesque No. 1. Claude Debussy

Greatest Love of All. Whitney Houston

 ## 4. POLYDYNAMICS

Usually, there are multiple dynamic levels present in any given piece of music. Notice how one of the melodies stands out above the others; it is called the prominent melody.

Suggestion for Additional Listening:

Prelude in G minor, Opus 23, No. 5, middle section. S. Rachmaninoff

Any piece by Chopin or Brahms

More often than not, melodies shift in their relative importance. If you find yourself listening to one melody now, and then another during the same piece of music, you are experiencing one of the principal beauties of music—the shifting of emphasis from one voice part to another. It's amusing to see and hear how a prominent melody is distributed from one instrument to another during an orchestral performance (Figure **5.6**).

FIGURE 5.6 Grand Festival of Russian National Orchestra in Tchaikovsky Concert Hall, Moscow, September 8, 2012.

TEXTURE

Musical texture refers to the number of voice parts and relationships between them.

 ### 1. MONOPHONIC (ONE VOICE PART)

Sometimes a folk singer sings without playing his guitar. When he sings alone, without accompaniment, the music is called monophonic (music with only one voice part). Even if others join in and sing the same melody the music is still be labeled monophonic. It does not matter how many people are singing—if they all sing the same tune at the same time, and on the same pitches, the music is monophonic.

Suggestion for Additional Listening:

Don McLean singing the opening of *American Pie*

 ### 2. HOMOPHONIC (CHORDS AND MELODY)

Whenever a singer strums chords on his guitar while singing, or plays chords on a piano, the musical effect is labeled homophonic. Homophonic music occurs when chords accompany a melody.

Suggestion for Additional Listening:

Don McLean singing the opening of *American Pie* while strumming on his guitar

 ### 3. POLYPHONIC (SINGING IN ROUNDS)

Poly means many; polyphonic means many melodies at once. The easiest way to understand polyphony is to remember how you sing camp songs as rounds.

One group starts to sing—	**Row, Row, Row your boat...**
another group chimes in—	**Row, Row, Row your boat...**
and another group follows	**Row, Row, Row your boat your boat,**
	gently down the stream....

until the entire piece spins out to the end as polyphonic music. The chief characteristic of polyphonic music is staggered entries and overlapping voices. When you hear simultaneous, independent melodies, you are listening to the polyphony of music.

Suggestion for Additional Listening:

"Little" *Fugue in G minor.* J. S. Bach

FIGURE 5.7 *Invention in the Style of J.S. Bach* (measures 1-4),

 A special kind of polyphonic music called *fugue* has strict rules about how voices may begin and follow each other. Each voice part has a special name and the procedures used to link them together follow strict rules. A musical score shown in Figure **5.7** presents the main tune or (subject) and its "answer" enclosed in rectangles. This piece has just two voice parts that chase after each other. Similar pieces can have as many as five voice parts—all based upon the same melody. You can listen to the music shown in Figure **5.7** by visiting the following YouTube address:

http://www.youtube.com/watch?v=8FWHJbRqRUQ .

♪ 4. HETEROPHONIC

Heterophonic music is a circumstance where one melody is a decorated version of another. This technique is often found in folk and tribal music of the world.

Suggestion for Additional Listening:

Natalie Cole singing "Unforgettable" with her father Nat "King" Cole

ADDITIONAL TEXTURE TERMS

Four more terms are added here in order to expand your ability to identify sounds and improve your skill at discussing music. The terms are density, blend, register, and range.

Density

Density is the number of instruments or melodic lines present in a musical example. A thin texture has few instruments; a thick texture has many instruments.

1. LOW DENSITY

A thin texture with few instruments

Suggestion for Additional Listening:

Any classical chamber work

Can you name a piece of music that has just a few instruments? _____

2. HIGH DENSITY

A thick texture with many instruments

Suggestion for Additional Listening:

Fifth movement, *Symphonie Fantastique*. Hector Berlioz

Any of the *Star Wars* films

Can you name a piece with a whole orchestra playing? _____

Blend

Blend is the degree to which instrumental or vocal sounds appear to overlap. Often, voices in a Renaissance choir are barely distinguishable from each other because the music has close blend. On the other hand, music by a contemporary rock ensemble may have easily distinguishable instruments, or open blend.

1. CLOSE BLEND

Voice parts are barely distinguishable from each other in much Renaissance choral music.

Suggestion for Additional Listening:

"Tu Solus." vocal motet. Josquin Des Pres

Can you name a piece with close blend? _____

2. OPEN BLEND

Voice parts are easily distinguishable from each other in most Rock music.

Suggestions for Additional Listening:

Octet for Winds, 1923. Igor Stravinsky

In America. Charlie Daniels band

Can you name a piece with open blend? _____

Register

Register refers to the general pitch level of the music. Sometimes a musical excerpt is in a high register and sometimes it is in a low register. In an opera where a character dies and goes to Heaven, you might expect the music to be in the high register. In an opera example where someone is mortally wounded, however, you might expect the music to be in the low register. Generally, the register of the music varies from one pitch area to another in order to avoid boredom.

♪ 1. HIGH REGISTER

Predominantly high notes in a musical example.

Suggestion for Additional Listening:

Almost any piece played by "101 Strings"

Can you name a piece with mainly high notes? _____

♪ 2. LOW REGISTER

Predominantly low notes in a musical example.

Suggestion for Additional Listening:

Opening of final act, *Tristan und Isolde*. Richard Wagner

Can you name a piece with mainly low notes? _____

Range

Range comprises the upper and lower pitch boundaries of musical texture. A narrow range involves a limited sound bandwidth and might be as simple as a conjunct melody, while a wide range involves a broad spectrum of pitches. "Luke's Theme" from John Williams' *Star Wars*, has not only instruments playing many pitches (full orchestra), but a tune that has a wide range and is disjunct (see Melody above).

♪ 1. WIDE RANGE

Melodies with full orchestra

Suggestion for Additional Listening:

"Organ" *Symphony No. 3*," final movement, C. Saint Saens

Can you name some music with a wide range? _____

♪ 2. NARROW RANGE

Melodies bunched together within a narrow range.

Suggestion for Additional Listening:

The "theme" of any Theme and Variations.

Can you name a melody with a narrow range? _____

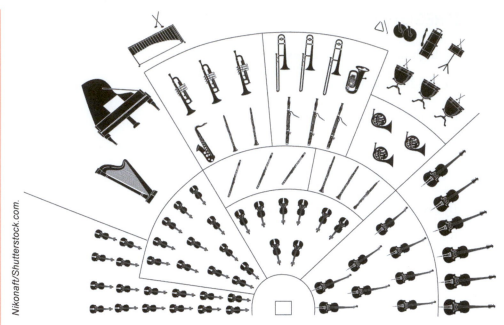

FIGURE 5.8 Instruments of the orchestra

TIMBRE

Musical timbre is the choice of instruments in a musical selection. Four string players are performing chamber music in Figure **5.3**. One can almost imagine the sound of this group in one's mind. The general sound of the group revolves around tiny details of each musical note played—their partials (or overtones), and their waveform envelope that collectively result in sound colors called "timbre." Once you understand the nature of timbre, you will be in a better position to be able to distinguish not only between instruments of the orchestra (Figure **5.8**), but instruments from around the world.

Timbre (pronounced tam burr) is a French word that essentially refers to the specific instrument(s) you hear. A more technical definition of this word would be the "waveform envelope and overtones" present in any given musical tone.

When a musician plays one note on his instrument, s/he actually plays many notes—a sound package of information.

Harmonic Series

Just one second in the life of two piano notes is shown in the diagram of Figure **5.9**. The computer sampled the sound from the lowest to the highest frequency in fractions of a second and produced jagged lines representing the intensities of various frequencies present in the sound. When these samples are lined up in parallel rows, the resulting diagram appears as a 3D landscape or sound scape. Notice that the initial strike of the hammer (far upper left side of the picture) is very loud—you can see large jagged pyramid where the notes rise up quickly—and also the aftermath as the pyramid declines and the notes die away.

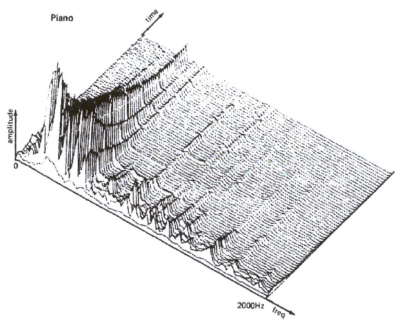

Piano

time

amplitude

0

2000Hz   freq

Martin Piszczalski and Bernard A. Galler, 'Automatic Music Transcription', Computer Music Journal, 1:4 (November, 1977), pp. 24–31. © 19797 by The MIT Press.

FIGURE 5.9 Martin Piszczalski, "Spectral Surfaces from Performed Music, Part 2," *Computer Music Journal* (November, 1977), p. 24.

Also, notice that there are many other smaller peaks to the right and bottom of the illustration indicating the presence of other notes. These extra peaks or ragged edges are called overtones, partials, or spectral components (depending on whether you are a musician or a physicist).

Musical notes are sound packages containing one loud low note (the fundamental, shown as a large peak in the illustration) and many other softer notes called partials. If the partials are stripped away from a note, it will start to sound like another instrument—or change its *timbre*. This explains why a note played on a piano sounds completely different from the same note played on a clarinet or some other instrument. All instruments have different partials or overtones for the same note.

ACTIVITY

1. Form your lips into a circle and sing "ooooh."
2. Continue to sing and slowly open your mouth.

   The sound will change from oooooooh to waaahhh and this will result in a change in timbre because the opening of your mouth has re-shaped the sound amplifier (mouth cavity) to produce new partials.

Musical Notes as Sound Packages

 ### 1. HARMONIC SOUNDING INSTRUMENTS

Harmonic instruments—having just a few of the harmonic series in their upper partials—sound more like a whistle [or flute] and have little noise content.

Suggestion for Additional Listening:

Any piece featuring a flute

 ### 2. INHARMONIC OR NOISY INSTRUMENTS

If odd or assorted partials are introduced into the waveform envelope, however, the note will sound "noisy" or inharmonic. Inharmonic instruments such as a kazoo or bassoon have a buzzing sound to them; they are noisy. Noise is not the same as volume. When someone asks you if an instrument is noisy, you should base your judgment upon how inharmonic it sounds, not how loud it is.

Suggestion for Additional Listening:

A bagpipe

Waveform Envelope

In addition to the partials (and much easier to understand), musical notes have an attack character. There are three stages in the life of any single note: attack, sustain, and decay as shown in Figure **5.10.**

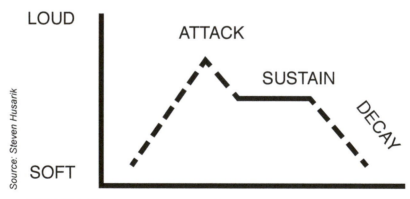

FIGURE 5.10 Attack and Decay Character of a Single Note

♪ 3. HARD OR SHARP ATTACK

Different instruments have different waveform envelopes. Instruments like pianos that strike notes have a sharp or hard attack. Gongs, bells, and other hammered instruments have hard attacks. Some instruments have sharp attacks without the long decay character of a bell. The old-fashioned typewriter occurs as a percussion instrument in some modern musical compositions. A typewriter click is abrupt, but there is no sustain or decay. One hears its initial attack and then the sound quickly disappears.

Suggestion for Additional Listening:

Any piano piece

♪ 4. SOFT ATTACK

Instruments like a pipe organ or a flute have a soft attack.

Suggestion for Additional Listening:

Any pipe organ piece

♪ 5. LONG DECAY

Instruments such as gongs have a hard attack, but also a long sustain and decay period—you can hear them ringing long after they have been struck.

Suggestion for Additional Listening:

Any composition with gongs or any piece played on a bell tower

Can you name some instruments with a sharp attack? _____

Can you name some instruments with a long decay? _____

Can you name some instruments with a short decay? _____

Non-Western Instrumentation

At one time it was customary to identify instruments by their location in the Western orchestra. Nowadays, an ethnomusicological approach assigns instruments to categories that suit the music of non-Western cultures:

♪ **1. Idiophones** (struck instruments).

♪ **2. Chordophones** (instrument with a string).

♪ **3. Membranophones** (instruments with a stretched skin).

♪ **4. Aerophones** (instruments with a vibrating column of air).

♪ **5. Electrophones** (electronically driven instruments).

CRITICAL METHOD APPLICATION

Apply the Critical Method to Beyonce's work, *Formation*. Remember, as discussed in Chapter One, the steps include Description, Analysis, Interpretation, and Evaluation.

DESCRIPTION

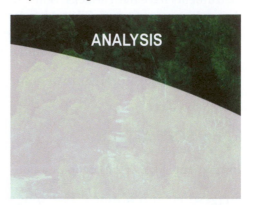

ANALYSIS

INTERPRETATION

EVALUATION

CRITICAL TERMS

ELEMENTS OF MUSIC

MELODY	Succession of organized pitches
HARMONY	Dissonant and consonant progress of chords
RHYTHM	Organization of sound with pulse beats
DYNAMICS	Loudness, softness, and all degrees in between
TEXTURE	Interaction of melodies
TIMBRE	Choice of instrument, attack and upper partials

ADDITIONAL TERMS

Melody

CONJUNCT	Melody hovers around the same few notes
DISJUNCT	Melody contains leaps upward or downward
MELISMATIC	Many notes for each syllable
SYLLABIC	One note for each syllable

Harmony

CONSONANCE	Pleasant sound of simultaneous pitches located three notes apart
DISSONANCE	Harsh sound of notes placed close together
HARMONIC RHYTHM	Rate of chord change
MAJOR MODE	Happy sounding piece
MINOR MODE	Sad sounding piece

Rhythm

FAST PULSE	Upbeat tempo
NO PULSE	No detectable beat
RUBATO	Beat speeds up and slows down
SLOW PULSE	Slow beat
STRONG PULSE	Foot stomping beat

Dynamics

DYNAMIC CURVE	Slowing getting louder or softer
FORTE	High level of loudness
POLYDYNAMICS	Many dynamic levels at once
PIANO	Low level of loudness
TERRACE	Stratification of dynamic levels by adding instruments

Texture

BLEND	Instrumental overlap forming a coherent sonority
DENSITY	Number of instruments or melodic lines
HOMOPHONY	Melody plus chords
MONOPHONY	One melodic line
POLYPHONY	Melodies in rounds
RANGE	Pitch boundary of a musical texture
REGISTER	Pitch level of an ensemble or part

Timbre

ATTACK	Beginning of the sound
DECAY	End of the sound
HARMONIC SERIES	Naturally occurring notes above a fundamental
HARMONIC INSTRUMENTS	Flute-like sounds
INHARMONIC INSTRUMENTS	Raspy sounding instruments
SUSTAIN	Time between the attack and decay
WAVEFORM ENVELOPE	Amplitude, pitches and length of a sound

REVIEW QUESTION

♪ **REVIEW QUESTION**: A musical example lasting one minute is given in the sound file. Please list all of the terms that apply to this example, or another musical example of your choice.

CRITICAL COMMENTARY

The skill of identifying sounds seems almost magical to some people. Applying musical terms to sounds causes the magic to disappear, however, and enables the listener to unmask the mysteries of music. Technical terminology puts one on the same footing as professionals in the field and enables one to discuss and evaluate sounds as effectively as any other art object.

LITERATURE
LYRIC/EPIC

"A rose is a rose is a rose."
—Gertrude Stein (1874–1946)

TYPES OF POETRY

Language and music are closely connected and, apart from the singing of musical *recitative* in opera, poetry is perhaps the closest marriage of the two art forms. Some of the greatest pieces of literature (e.g., *Iliad/Odyssey*) derive from the singing of tales. As an arrangement of language, poetry is capable of revealing the world of personality, emotion, and sound pattern. The three types poetry include lyric, narrative, and dramatic.

LYRIC POETRY

Lyric poetry is defined as a short sung verse, traditionally with both rhythm and rhyme. The root word of lyric is *lyre* suggesting that the Ancient Greeks sang these poems accompanied by an instrument called a *lyre*—a cross between a harp and a guitar.

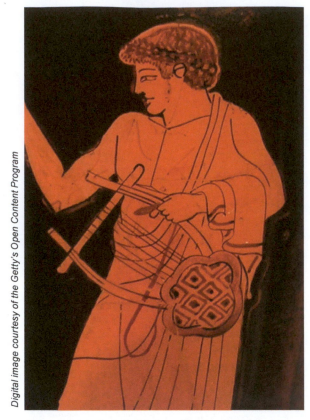

FIGURE 6.1 *Detail, Oil Jar with Man Holding a Lyre* (ca. 480 B.C.E.). Getty Villa Museum, Malibu, CA

The popular counterpart of this art form today can be found in the songs of Don McLean such as *American Pie* (1971). It is difficult to think of the words of this iconic song without imagining the musical notes that go with it.

If one had never heard the music that accompanies this lyric, it would be difficult to understand why it has become an America icon. Imagine how difficult it is, then, to appreciate lyric poetry of the Ancient Greeks without knowing the music that accompanies the repertory. As well, a considerable loss of effect is experienced when sentences are translated into modern language—leaving only a shell of the original as an arrangement of language.

EPIC POETRY

Epic poetry tells a story that is both spoken and sung to an audience. The great epic poems *Iliad* and *Odyssey* were originally compilations of folk stories that provided entertainment to people before there were any electronic media, radio, television, video, or computers. Listeners at the time eagerly listened to these poetic tales re-told sometimes to the sound of a stringed or wind accompaniment. The tradition lingers today in the singing of old Gallic legends in the pubs of Ireland or in Turkish village inns where one can hear old tales sung by locals playing folk instruments. Aural (sound) and oral (voice) traditions combine to preserve people's culture through these epic tales.

Here is a quotation of the famous opening lines from Book 2 of the *Odyssey*, the celebrated ancient epic by Homer:

Excerpt, *Odyssey*, Homer

As soon as rosey-fingered early Dawn appeared,
Odysseus' dear son jumped up out of bed and dressed.
He slung a sharp sword from his shoulders, then laced
his lovely sandals over his shining feet . . . .

Certainly the descriptive terms and arrangement of language found in this translated excerpt are fascinating, but can you imagine this narrative in its original speech rhythms? Can you imagine it with music? The effect must have been captivating for listeners many centuries ago.

DRAMATIC POETRY

Dramatic poetry occurs in plays. Good examples of dramatic poetry are found in the soliloquies of Shakespeare's plays. A soliloquy is a section of a play where a character talks aloud and reveals his innermost thoughts—thereby giving the audience superior knowledge over the characters in a play. In this excerpt from Shakespeare's *Hamlet* (1603/ 1623), the main character reveals his innermost thoughts and debates a course of action.

Excerpt, *Hamlet*, William Shakespeare

To be, or not to be—that is the question:
Whether 'tis nobler in the mind to suffer
The slings and arrows of outrageous fortune
Or to take arms against a sea of troubles . . . .

Soliloquies are comparable to voice-overs in films such as *Platoon*, where the main character Chris reads letters from the Viet Nam battlefield in a voice over to his grandmother at home. The audience knows his innermost feelings and understands his point of view better than any of his fellow soldiers, because they hear him reading his letters out loud.

ACTIVITY

Poetry is often treated as an arrangement of language today—sometimes even as oration. Public readers of poetry are performers who have a responsibility to define the form for their listeners; they must give appropriate attention to the pronunciation of vowels, hard and soft consonants, pauses, and hidden patterns that emphasize the rhythm of each line and structure of the poem. If these features are ignored the poetic reading may sound choppy, lack definition, or miss the intention of the author altogether.

We can easily forget how important pronunciation is until we are made aware of it by technology. Please go to the ATT Voice generator site given here and type in the excerpt from Shakespeare's *Sonnet No. 18* given below:

http://www2.research.att.com/~ttsweb/tts/demo.php

Select a "speaker" and listen to that electronic person read the sonnet to determine what details of speech are missing:

Excerpt, *Sonnet No. 18,* William Shakespeare

Shall I compare thee to a summer's day?
Thou art more lovely and more temperate.
Rough winds do shake the darling buds of May,
And summer's lease hath all too short a date…
But thy eternal summer shall not fade….
So long as men can breath or eyes can see,
So long lives this, and this gives life to thee.

Can you hear how the reading of this poem by a digital person is different from what you, yourself would do? The awkward inflections and inappropriate pauses in the electronic voice signal that this is a digitization rather than a real person. The automatic person is reading letters and syllables, but does not know what they mean. Reading poetry out loud to others requires understanding and attention to tiny details of speech called performance practices that are unique to each historical period and style of poetry.

Now, type a few lines of your favorite poem into the online voice generator and determine what is missing in the pronunciation of the computer voice that could give life to the lines of poetry. How would you misspell certain words and repeat letters in order to get the electronic voice to pronounce words more correctly? Could you influence the rise and fall of dramatic character in each line?

LYRIC POETRY

Ancient Greece

In any brief historical survey of poetry, Sappho would stand out as an important contributor to the art of the ancient world. Her poems exist today largely because other authors quoted them as exquisite models of lyric writing. Sappho came from the island of Lesbos and dedicated many of her poems to the pupils in her academy. Wealthy and widely traveled, she journeyed as far from home as Syracuse, Sicily. Although other writers proclaimed her as the greatest lyric poet, the few of her writings that survive have done so quite by accident. One poem written on parchment was found in the belly of a mummified crocodile.

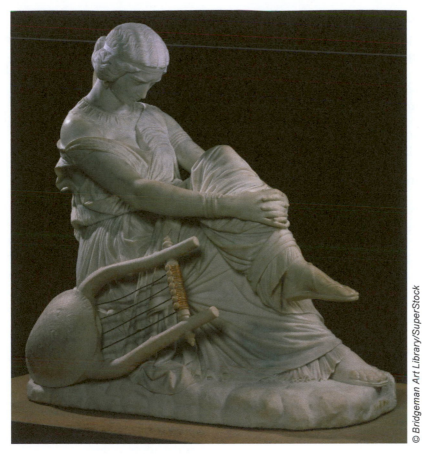

FIGURE 6.2 *Sappho with a turtle shell lyre* (1852), James Pradier. Musée D'Orsay, Paris

Because Sappho's poems are translated, they cannot be read in the original rhythm called sapphic meter. This meter consists of a series of shorts and longs (a long = two counts; a short = one count) as follows:

long-short, long-short,
long-short-short,
long-short, long-short

Thus, the poems are denuded of both their original melody, rhythm, and accompaniment when read in English. Once again, we can only appreciate them for their imagery and arrangement of language.

Hymn to Aphrodite

Subtle-bloomed, gold-throned
Aphrodite, deathless

child of Zeus, who braids clever nets,
I beg you

not to tame my languorous
heart's lamenting,

Desperately I ask you—

Come to me if ever you thought you
loved me,

ever heard the cry of my voice from
far-off.

Consenting, you left your father's home
in the sky

Coming to help.

Splendid swallows pulled on your
chariot's reins toward

freshly furrowed earth on their
thickly feathered

wings, and through ether, eddying
air, and swiftly

brought you to my side.

You arrived, most envied, most
happy goddess,

smiling, nearly laughing, and asked
me wryly

what on earth was wrong with me
this time, why

again had I called you.

What did I want most in my sickened
heart and

think should happen, "Who shall
Persuasion work to

coax for you, to lead by the hand to
your love?"

"Who, Sapph, has wronged you?"

[Note that Sappho is on
familiar terms with the
goddess Aphrodite, who
addresses her as "Sapph," not
with the formal "Sappho."]

"If she runs, then soon she shall chase
you, if she

won't accept your gifts, you'll refuse
her presents.

Though she hates you now, she will
soon adore you—

though unwillingly."

Come right now and free me from
the weight of

Heartache, please make everything
happen as I

want it, give me all I desire, and be my

ally in arms.

Translated by J'laine Vest. Courtesy of J'laine Vest.

Some of Sappho's poems appear as quatrains—four-line stanzas sometimes with a rhyming pattern.

Moon is Down

Moon is down,

The Pleiades. Midnight,

The hours flow on,

I lie, alone.

Renaissance

Although words and music were generally partners in Ancient Greek drama and verse, by the time of the Renaissance they were distinctly separate entities—where the words became primarily an arrangement of language without music. There was an attempt at the time to unite them in a style known as *recitative* (the driving force behind early opera), however, poetry continued as an arrangement of language in succeeding centuries.

Though today known primarily as a playwright, William Shakespeare, a late Renaissance writer, called himself a bard or poet to his friends (Figure **6.3**). Many of his expressions have crept into our modern language and we unwittingly take for granted

Georgios Kollidas/Shutterstock.com.

FIGURE 6.3 *William Shakespeare* (1564–1616). Engraved by E. Scriven (1835). The Gallery of Portraits with Memoirs Encyclopedia, United Kingdom

his contributions to the English language. His additions to our language include hundreds of words and expressions such as "fight fire with fire," "come what may," "love is blind," and "seen better days."

Shakespeare's sonnets employ formulas based upon the vowel sounds at the end of each line. In a typical Shakespearean sonnet, the first line ends with a sound that is unlike the second line, but is similar to the end of the third line. The second line ends with a sound that is unlike the third line, but is similar to the fourth line. These four lines comprise a quatrain, followed by two more quatrains, until the last two lines rhyme with each other as a couplet as shown below.

Shakespearean Sonnet Rhyme Scheme

AB quatrain
AB

CD quatrain
CD

EF quatrain
EF

GG couplet

One of the interesting poetic structures employed during Shakespeare's time was the *conceit*—an extended metaphor comparing two persons, subjects, or states of being. A *conceit* is not just a short comparison, but one that occupies a significant portion of the poem. In *Sonnet No. 60*, Shakespeare compares our lives to the waves of water working their way up to the edge of a shoreline. He then waxes poetically about how age destroys youthful beauty. The *conceit* in this example is shown in bold letters.

Sonnet No. 60, William Shakespeare

	[Rhyme Scheme]
Like as the waves make towards the pebbled shore,	[A]
So do our minutes hasten to their end;	[B]
Each changing place with that which goes before,	[A]
In sequent toil all forwards do contend.	[B]
Nativity, once in the main of light,	[C]
Crawls to maturity, wherewith being crown'd,	[D]
Crooked eclipses 'gainst his glory fight,	[C]
And Time that gave, doth now his gift confound.	[D]
Time doth transfix the flourish set on youth	[E]
And delves the parallels in beauty's brow,	[F]
Feeds on the rarities of nature's truth,	[E]
And nothing stands but for his scythe to mow;	[F]
And yet to times in hope my verse shall stand,	[G]
Praising thy worth, despite his cruel hand.	[G]

A younger contemporary of Shakespeare, John Donne (1572-1631), wrote a poem for his wife entitled *A Valediction Forbidding Mourning*. Donne (Figure **6.4**) describes the strength of their love and compares both of them to the feet of a compass (Figure **6.5**). He extends this comparison into a *conceit* (shown in bold letters) where he and his wife become the two points or feet of the compass moving in relationship to each other. Once again, the *conceit* is shown with bold letters.

Ipsumpix/Getty Images

FIGURE 6.4 John Donne, by an Unknown English artist, oil on panel (ca. 1595). National Portrait Gallery, London

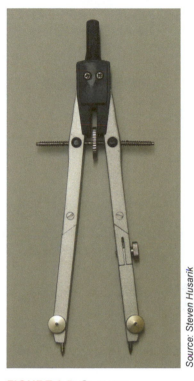

Source: Steven Husarik

FIGURE 6.5 *Compass*

A Valediction Forbidding Mourning, John Donne

As virtuous men passe mildly away

    And whisper to their soules, to goe,

Whilst some of their sad friends doe say,

    The breath goes now, and some say, no.

So let us melt, and make no noise

    No teare-floods, nor sigh-tempests move,

T'were prophanation of our joyes

    To tell the layetie our love.

Moving of th' earth brings harmes and fears,

    Men reckon what it did and meant,

But trepidation of the spheares,

    Though greater farre, is innocent.

Dull sublunary lovers love

    (Whose soule is sense) cannot admit

Absence, because it doth remove

    Those things which elemented it.

But we by' a love, so much refin'd

    That our selves know not what it is,

Inter-assured of the mind,

    Care lesse, eyes, lips, and hands to misse.

Our two souls therefore, which are one,

    Though I must goe, endure not yet

A breach, but an expansion,

    Like gold to ayery thinnesse beate.

If they be two, they are two so

    As stiffe twin compasses are two,

Thy soule the fixt foot, makes no show

    To move, but doth, if the other doe.

And though it in the center sit,

    Yet when the other far doth rome,

It leanes, and hearkens after it,

    And growes erect, as that comes home.

Such wilt thou be to mee, who must

    Like th' other foot, obliquely runne.

Thy firmness makes my circle just,

    And makes me end, where I begunne.

Baroque (Figures of Speech)

One of the interesting developments of the Baroque era is the creation of expressive devices called "figures." There were catalogs of musical figures, visual figures, literary figures, dance figures, and even catalogs for military moves.

In music, the theory of *Affektenlehre* proposed that musical effects reduce to a collection of short musical motifs. A three-note group might express passion, another three-note group might express happiness, and another might express grace. By combining these musical figures a composer could create the music he desired for any situation.

In the visual arts, Charles LeBrun created an encyclopedia of facial expressions in his *Methode pour apprendre à dessiner les passions,* 1668. He illustrated faces showing ecstasy, contempt, horror, and hundreds of others for use by other artisans to make wall and ceiling paintings.

In ballet, various steps were crystallized into formulas at the school founded in the Palace of Versailles, France and choreographed to create interesting stage spectacles with music. A long tradition of ballet thus evolved from the court of Louis XIV in France that eventually led to 19th century ballet.

Baroque poets also constructed poems with literary figures. Some principal baroque figures of speech include oxymoron, antithesis, metaphor, simile, and anaphora.

One can better appreciate *The Flaming Heart upon the Book and Picture of St. Teresa* by John Crashaw by recognizing that figures of speech are riddled throughout the text. Let us define some Baroque figures of speech before reading it.

Oxymoron An oxymoron is the juxtaposition of words with contrary or opposite meaning such as sweet pain. (Pain is not very sweet.) Others include "sweet sorrow," "deafening silence," "military intelligence," or the television series called "Amish Mafia."

Antithesis Antitheses are contrasting ideas (they convey opposite meanings) in balanced phrases. For example, "The wounded is the wounding heart." Is the heart wounding someone or has it been wounded by someone? There is an opposition in the sentence structure and contradiction in meaning. Another example would be "I would and would not; I am on fire yet dare not." In other words, the person is motivated to do something, yet, is not motivated at all. Perhaps the most famous antithesis occurs in Lincoln's Gettysburg Address: "The world will little note nor long remember what we said here but it cannot long forget what they did here."

Metaphor A metaphor is an analogy between two persons, subjects, or states of being. For example, "the evening of life" suggests that a person's life can be compared to the times of day such as the morning of life, the afternoon of life, and the evening of life. Some other metaphors include, "fame is a bubble," "in the jaws of death," or "architecture is frozen music."

Simile A simile is similar to a metaphor except that it employs the words "like" or "as": "my life is like a red rose," "she has cheeks like roses," "he eats like a horse," and "cornered like a rat."

Anaphora The anaphora is the repetition of the same word(s) at the beginning of two or more lines of a poem. For example, "to the road...., to the house....to grandmother's house...etc. It is almost the reverse of a rhyme scheme—instead of the rhyme occurring at the end of the line, it occurs at the beginning.

It is difficult to separate secular and sacred aspects of love in Crashaw's metaphysical poem. Built around a *conceit* of "the hunt," the author is depicted as having been slain by love on love's property. Love takes arrows out of his quiver and then shoots the person through the heart. The slain person lies dead out in the field like a dead deer ("a carcass of a cold, hard hart"), a victim of love's attack. The love-slain victim is then gutted by love as if the victim of a physical slaying. In certain respects, this is a violent poem. Have you ever experienced a powerful love break up that has left you weary and depleted like the author of this poem?

Source: Steven Husarik

FIGURE 6.6 *Ecstasy of Santa Teresa* (1647–52), Gian Lorenzo Bernini. Cornaro Chapel, Santa Maria della Victoria, Rome

Excerpt, *The Flaming Heart* (1652), Richard Crashaw

The Rosie hand, the flaming Heart

Leave Her alone The Flaming Heart.

   Leave her that; and thou shalt leave her

Not one loose shaft but love's whole quiver.

For in love's field was never found

A nobler weapon than a Wound.

Love's passives are his activ'st part.

The wounded is the wounding heart.

O Heart! the equal poise of love's both parts

Big alike with wounds and darts.

Live in these conquering leaves; live all the same;

And walk through all tongues one triumphant Flame.

Live here, great Heart; and love and die and kill;

And bleed and wound; and yield and conquer still.

Let this immortal life where'er it comes

Walk in a crowd of loves and Martyrdoms.

Let mystic Deaths wait on it; and wise souls be

The love-slain witnesses of this life of thee.

O sweet incendiary! show here thy art,

Upon this carcass of a hard, cold hart.

Let all thy scatter'd shafts of light, that play

Among the leaves of thy large books of day;

Combin'd against this Breast at once break in

And take away from me my self and sin,

This gracious Robbery shall thy bounty be;

And my best fortunes such fair spoils of me.

O thou undaunted daughter of desires!

By all the dower of Lights and Fires;

By all the eagle in thee, all the dove;

By all they lives and deaths of love;

By the large draughts of intellectual day,

And by thy thirsts of love more large than they;

By all thy brim-fill'd Bowls of fierce desire

By thy last Morning's draught of liquid fire;

By the full kingdom of that final kiss

That seiz'd thy parting Soul, and seal'd thee his;

By all the heav'ns thou hast in him

(Fair sister of the Seraphim!)

By all of Him we have in Thee;

Let me so read thy life, that I

Unto all life of mine may die.

ACTIVITY

In order to appreciate the dense beauty of this poem one must consider its decorative use of figures of speech. Please locate as many Baroque figures of speech in Crashaw's poem as possible.

Modern Poets

Numerous movements appeared in the early 20th century whose names end with the suffix "ism" and each of them is a reaction of the artistic past: surrealism, fauvism, cubism, pointillism, and expressionism. One might go so far as to say that "ism" translates as, "I dislike the past." These movements comprise what we call today the Modern world.

In particular, the writers who gathered in Paris, France at Sylvia Beach's bookstore shown in Figure **6.7** formed a circle that gave rise to many literary experiments leading to Modernism in literature. Now known as *Shakespeare and Co.* (Figure **6.8**) the bookstore moved to its new location after WWII.

FIGURE 6.7 Sylvia Beach's original bookstore, 12 Rue de l'Odéon, Paris

FIGURE 6.8 Shakespeare and Company, opened in 1951, 37 Rue de la Bûcherie, Paris

Source: Steven Husarik

Many expatriate poets met at Ms. Beach's bookstore principally because they felt unappreciated at home—particularly those from the United States. The group included Gertrude Stein, F. Scott Fitzgerald, Ezra Pound, and James Joyce. Some unique literary styles resulted from their experiments such as stream of consciousness technique (e.g., found in James Joyce's "Mollie's Monologue," from *Ulysses*), and cubist writing style.

Stream of Consciousness

Ulysses, James Joyce (1880–1941)

Ulysses is the story of all the events and characters in one day of the life of one man. As we break into the story at the end, Mollie, the temptress, is daydreaming and her thoughts are presented in sentences that run together without punctuation and capitalization—in much the same way the human mind thinks.

Contrary to those who believe that human thought is constructed in conventional sentences, the human mind does not need punctuation to think. It moves far more freely and elegantly than written language, and can change direction in a split second. The mind can even think about two different things at once. Periods, commas, and capital letters are trivial constructs in the environment of a thinking human brain.

FIGURE 6.9 *Algeciras, Spain*, viewed from *Rock of Gibraltar* and referred to in "Mollie's Monologue," *Ulysses*. The Alameda Gardens are at the bottom of the photo.

When an author such as Joyce elects to avoid capitals, periods, commas, and other punctuation marks, however, new techniques are needed to create a sense of closure. Please note how the word "yes" occurs more frequently toward the end of *Mollie's monolog*—almost imitating the sequence of rhythmic accents occurring in a bouncing ball as it comes to rest, Yes…Yes…Yes… Joyce creates a new technique for controlling action by repeating the single word "Yes" logarithmically at the end of the text.

Episode 18 (finale): "Mollie's Monologue" from *Ulysses* by James Joyce

....Ill have him eyeing up at the ceiling where is she gone now make him want me that's the only way a quarter after what an unearthly hour I suppose theyre just getting up in China now combing out their pigtails for the day well soon have the nuns ringing the angelus theyve nobody coming in to spoil their sleep except an old priest or two for his night office the alarm clock next door at cockshout clattering the brains out of itself let me see if I can doze off 1 2 3 4 5 what kind of flowers are those they invented like the stars the wallpaper in Lombard Street was much nicer the apron he gave me was like that something only I only wore it twice better lower this lamp and try again so as I can get up early Ill go to Lambes there beside Find-laters and get them to send us some flowers to put about the place in case he brings him home tomorrow today I mean no no Fridays an unlucky day first I want to do the place up someway the dust grows in it I think while I'm asleep then we can have music and cigarettes I can accompany him first I must clean the keys of the piano with milk whatll I wear shall I wear a white rose or those fairy cakes in Liptons I love the smell of a rich big shop at 71/2d. a lb or the other ones with the cherries in them and the pinky sugar 11d. a couple of lbs of course a nice plant for the middle of the table Id get that cheaper in wait wheres this I saw them not long ago I love flowers Id love to have the whole place swimming in roses God of heaven theres nothing like nature the wild mountains then the sea and the waves rushing then the beautiful country with fields of oats and all kinds of things and all the fine cattle going about that would do your heart good to see rivers and lakes and flowers all sorts of shapes and smells and colours springing up even out of the ditches primroses and violets nature it is for them saying theres no God I wouldnt give a snap of my two fingers for all their learning why don't they go and create something I often asked him atheists or whatever they call themselves go and wash the cobbles off themselves first then go howling for the priest and they dying and why why because theyre afraid of hell on account of their bad conscience ah yes I know them well who was the first person in the universe before there was anybody that made it all who ah that they dont know neither do I so there you are they might as well try to stop the sun from rising tomorrow the sun shines for you he said the day we were lying among the rhododendrons on Howth head in the grey tweed suit and his straw hat the day I got him to propose to me yes first (I gave him the bit of seedcake out of my mouth and it was leapyear like now yes 16 years ago my God after that long kiss I near lost my breath yes he said I was a flower of the mountain yes so we are flowers all a womans body yes that was one true thing he said in his life and the sun shines for you today yes that was why I liked him because I saw he understood or felt what a woman is and I knew I could always get round him and I gave him all the pleasure I could leading him on till he asked me to say yes) and I wouldnt answer first only looked out over the sea and the sky I was thinking of so many things he didn't know of Mulvey and Mr Stanhope and Hester and father and old captain Groves and the sailors playing all birds fly and I say stoop and washing up dishes they called it on the pier and the sentry in front of the governors house with the thing round his white helmet poor devil half roasted and the Spanish girls laughing in their shawls and their tall combs and the auctions in the morning the Greeks and the jews and the Arabs and the devil knows who else from all the ends of Europe and Duke street and the fowl market all clucking outside Larby Sharons and the poor donkeys slipping half asleep and the vague fellows in the cloaks asleep in the shade on the steps and the big wheels of the carts of the bulls and the old castle thousands of years old yes and those handsome Moors all in white and turbans like kings asking you to sit down in their little bit of a shop and Ronda with the old windows of the posadas glancing eyes a lattice hid for her lover to kiss the iron and the wineshops half open at night and the castanets and the night we missed the boat at Algeciras the watchman going about serene with his lamp and O that awful deep-down torrent O and the sea the sea crimson sometimes like fire and the glorious sunsets and the figtrees in the Alameda gardens yes and all the queer little streets and pink and blue and yellow houses and the rosegardens and the jessamine and geraniums and cactuses and Gibraltar as a girl where I was a Flower of the mountain yes when I put the rose in my hair like the Andalusian girls used or shall I wear a red yes and how he kissed me under the Moorish wall and I thought well as well him as another and then I asked him with my eyes to ask again yes and then he asked me would I yes to say yes my mountain flower and first I put my arms around him yes and drew him down to me so he could feel my breasts all perfume yes and his heart was going like mad and yes I said yes I will Yes.

ACTIVITY

Please select a moment of thought from your mind and write it down verbatim as a stream of consciousness lyric. What does this fragment of your thought process tell about your personality and the way you think? How might you publish this excerpt of your thoughts to others?

EPIC LITERATURE

The epic is one of the most interesting forms of literature in the West. Not all countries have epics. China, for example, has only a limited epic tradition; efforts are currently underway to document many African stories formerly told only through song. Originally, epics were sung stories collected over the centuries and preserved by oral tradition. Some of the famous literary epics from the West are shown in the table below.

Famous Epics in the Western Tradition

Ancient Greece:	*Iliad/Odyssey* by Homer
Ancient Rome:	*Aeneid* by Virgil
Middle Ages:	*Beowolf; Nibelungenlied; The Comedy*, by Dante
Renaissance:	*The Faerie Queen* by Spencer; *Paradise Lost* by Milton
20th Century:	*Star Wars* by Lucas

The inclusion of *Star Wars* (1977) in this list may give pause to purists; however, this modern epic has pedagogical advantages. It is generally easier to remember the characteristics of epics if we attach them to a well-known contemporary model.

Characteristics of Epics

Long narrative poem	Adventure and action
Many episodes [stories within a story]	Covers much geography
Takes place outside of real time	Characters of stature, wealth, power
Gods, goddesses	Man searching for values [roots]
Escapism-fantasy	Shows conflict between good and evil
Based on myth and legend	Grand style, eloquent
Early examples were sung	Previous history, culture and religious ideas

"a long time ago, in another galaxy far, far, away...." Star Wars

Star Wars is a long, narrative poem, full of action, adventure, escapism, and fantasy. It covers much geography (indeed, all the galaxies), and includes characters of wealth, stature (Princess Leia), and power (Darth Vader). It has many episodes (stories within stories); six in all, the most famous of which is *Episode 4, A New Hope*. The story takes place outside of real time "a long time ago, in another galaxy far, far, away..." and is organized around the idea of a man (Luke) searching for values (searching for his roots). These stories typically show the conflict between good (The Force) and evil (The Dark side of the Force). Finally, like other literary epics, this story incorporates myth and legend. Let us define those two terms before turning to the story itself.

Legend

A legend is a story based in truth, but distorted over time. Legends are somewhat like the parlor game of Telephone where someone whispers something in one person's ear and that person whispers what they heard into their neighbor's ear—all the way around a circle—until the original person announces to the group what s/he heard. The distortions are quite amusing, which is why Telephone is a good parlor game.

ACTIVITY

Name some legendary characters out of the old American west.

Famous legendary characters from the Old West in America such as Johnny Appleseed, Daniel Boone, Wyatt Earp, etc. are distorted in much the same way as messages in the game of Telephone. Johnny Appleseed supposedly planted apple trees all over the South (how many, and where is unclear). Daniel Boone seemingly killed a Grizzly bear with a knife (a singularly difficult task since Grizzly bears can suddenly explode into 30 miles per hour speed when caught off guard). How these people achieved such things is inexplicable, except that the stories are probably exaggerated. Modern celebrities such as Elvis Presley, Marilyn Monroe, and James Dean are becoming larger than life in the same manner—postage stamps have their portraits. We may never know the true stories about these people because they have become icons—legendary characters from Hollywood in the 1950s.

Myth

Myth is defined as a false story that is accepted as truth usually to explain away some natural phenomenon. For example, a person from the distant past might exclaim "It's thundering; the Gods are upset" because s/he thought there was a relationship between natural sounds and the attitudes of Gods. We have all heard of famous mythological figures from the past such as *Wodin*, *Thor*, or the *Cyclops*. They are mythological creations.

ACTIVITY

Name some famous mythological heroes from American comic books.

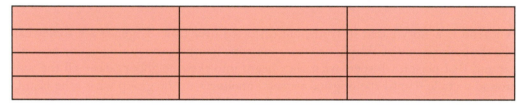

American mythology originates in comic book literature of the mid-1930s and 1940s, such as *Superman*, *Batman*, *Green Hornet*, and *Wonder Woman*. Our contemporary audience knows that there are no such characters, but accepts them for the sake of the story. Many of the films produced over the past twenty years are revivals of comic book characters and their stories.

Is there a mythical character in *Star Wars?* Yes, Chewbacca. It is said that one day while driving in the 1970s, a friend of George Lucas asked him whether he was going to put a *Wookiee* in his science fiction film. "What's a *Wookiee*?" Lucas supposedly asked. The person replied that a *Wookiee* is a half-man, half-beast in science fiction literature of the 1930s and 1940s that always growls, but everyone seems to know what he is saying. Lucas allegedly wrote down the word *Wookiee*, and *Chewbacca* later turned up in his film. Thus, *Star Wars* includes a character taken from American comic book mythology.

Returning to the list of characteristics of *epics* found in *Star Wars*, another important characteristic is that they were originally sung. This film is sung to the listeners, as well. John Williams used a special musical technique to compose the music for *Star Wars*, assigning a musical motif (or musical nametag) to each character such as Luke's theme, Obi-Wan Kenobi's theme, and Princess Leia's theme. Many people can sing Luke's theme from memory. Can you sing it from memory? As the story unfolds and events change, Luke's feelings change, and so his musical motif changes ever so slightly to fit the human emotions portrayed in the scene. Using a full symphony orchestra, the story is sung to the listener in a grand, eloquent style. In *Star Wars, Episode I*, an entire chorus joins up with the orchestra to sing the "tales of old."

Although *Star Wars* is not known as a literary epic, its narrative is published as a separate work and serves to illustrate the characteristics of famous epics.

CRITICAL METHOD APPLICATION

Apply the Critical Method to Shakespeare's work, *Sonnet 18*. Remember, as discussed in Chapter One, the steps include Description, Analysis, Interpretation, and Evaluation.

Excerpt, *Sonnet No. 18,* William Shakespeare

Shall I compare thee to a summer's day?
Thou art more lovely and more temperate.
Rough winds do shake the darling buds of May,
And summer's lease hath all too short a date…
But thy eternal summer shall not fade.…
So long as men can breath or eyes can see,
So long lives this, and this gives life to thee.

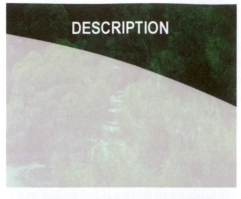

DESCRIPTION

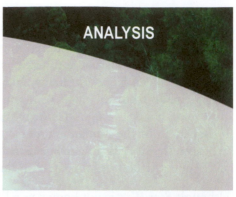

ANALYSIS

INTERPRETATION

EVALUATION

CRITICAL TERMS

TYPES OF POETRY

LYRIC	Short, sung poems
DRAMATIC	Verse that appears in a play (e.g., *soliloquy*)
NARRATIVE	Poems that tell a story; can be spoken or sung

SIX STRUCTURAL TECHNIQUES

ANAPHORA	Repetition of same word to introduce two or more lines
ANTITHESIS	Word groups conveying opposite meanings
METAPHOR	Analogy between two persons, subjects, states
OXYMORON	Juxtaposition of words with opposing meaning
SIMILE	Comparison of two things using the words "Like" or "As"

ADDITIONAL TERMS

CONCEIT	An extended metaphor
COUPLET	Pair of successive lines that rhyme and are of the same length
HARD CONSONANT	Consonants made up of clicks, pops, and fricatives
MODERNISM	Reaction to the past
QUATRAIN	Stanza or poem of four lines with alternate rhymes
SAPPHIC STANZA	Long-short, long-short, long-short-short, long-short, long-short
SHAKESPEARIAN SONNET	A B A B C D C D E F E F GG
SOFT CONSONANT	Consonants without noise
SOLILOQUY	Monologue where a character reveals his inner thoughts
STREAM OF CONSCIOUSNESS	Continuous unedited flow of thoughts through the mind

REVIEW QUESTION

"One whom some were certainly following was one who was completely charming. One whom some were certainly following was one who was charming. One whom some were following was one who was completely charming. One whom some were following was one who was certainly completely charming...."

The excerpt above is a good an example of

1. Antithesis
2. Simile
3. Metaphor
4. Anaphora
5. Oxymoron

Answer spelled backwards: arohpana

CRITICAL COMMENTARY

The study of poetry leads to greater understanding of literature and to the development of writing skills. Reading poems aloud also helps to develop analytical skills and performance practice skills. In addition, the study of poetry involves critical thought processes such as analysis, evaluation, and inference; it helps develop improved vocabulary, reading skills, phonetic understanding, and understanding of grammar.

DRAMA
A COMPOUND ART FORM

INTRODUCTION

Drama is a compound art form that requires not simply a text, but music, dance, and acting. Over the centuries, the development of staging, lighting and sound systems have all added to the art form. It is also important to note that the excerpt you will study in this chapter is more than a blueprint of the drama. Actors have to pronounce words with proper inflections; they must provide appropriate movements and gestures to bring the words to life. They have to interact with each other in a believable manner. Chorus members must sing, dance, and interact with the players, and the *aulos* player (Figure **7.2**) has to play at certain key points. There are staging and costume considerations, as well.

FIGURE 7.1 *Ancient Greek Theater* (ca. 4th century B.C.E.). Epidauros, Greece

ACTIVITY

Assume that you are a playwright who wishes to put on a successful play. List as many items as you can that are important to the production and then compare your list with the responses of others below.

PRACTICAL DRAMA REQUIREMENTS

VENUE/THEATER	DRESSING ROOMS	STAGE	ACTORS
DIRECTOR	CHOREOGRAPHER	STAGEHANDS	SCRIPT
PRODUCERS	MONEY	COSTUMES	ADVERTISEMENTS
PUBLICITY	TICKETS	PROGRAMS	AUDIENCE
PROPS	SOUND SYSTEM	LIGHTING	MUSIC

The reason you were asked to compile this list is to demonstrate that everything needed for a play today, was also needed twenty-eight centuries ago when the Ancient Greeks first produced drama of the sort we know today. Although there were earlier cultures who actually invented drama, our historical study emphasizes Western culture, and the Ancient Greek world is our starting point. Examine the list above and explain how each item needed today for productions compares with those needed from centuries ago.

ORIGINS OF DRAMA

There are at least two theories about the origin of drama in the West. According to one theory, drama originated with a single man named Thespis (hence, the term *Thespians*) who gave recitations and readings in temple complexes and was occasionally aided by an assistant.

If you travel in Greece and Turkey today, however, you will probably agree with the more widely accepted second theory that drama arose from religious ritual. There are dozens of Ancient Greek theaters in temple complexes that demonstrate how religious and medical rituals became manifest in physical structures. Let us proceed throug h the list of Practical Drama Requirements you compiled in order to see how drama arose from these theaters.

SPECTACLE

Theater

Ancient Greek theater design is comprised of three parts: *theatron*, *orchestra*, and *skene* (Figure **7.1**). The *theatron* is the semi-circular area for seating of the people. Below the *theatron* is a circular area called the *orchestra* where the action takes place and where an altar is located for sacrifices. An animal was originally slaughtered at the altar—but over time a character in a play was symbolically substituted. A special chair is located in the center front row for the priest of the cult who presided over these theatrical sacrifices. Thus, dramatic tragedies might be thought of as ritual sacrifices where a central character is held up for inspection and then metaphorically slaughtered at the altar in order to satisfy the gods.

Stage

The circular stage is located beneath the *theatron*, as opposed to the modern stage, which is sometimes raised above the audience.

Dressing Rooms/Skene (Scene)

A stage area called the *skene* is located behind the orchestra that contains dressing rooms and stage props. Occasionally on its front façade decorated panels indicate a locale.

Sound System

There was no need for a sound system in an Ancient Greek theater since the hillside auditorium was semi-circular in design and acoustically perfect. Buses pull up to the stage at *Epidauros* today and unload tourists who spill out and quickly run up to the top of the theater to whisper to the people down in the orchestra, "Can you hear me?" "Can you hear me?" Of course, their whispers can be heard distinctly because of the semi-circular acoustical design of the *theatron*.

Lighting

Lighting was not necessary in ancient plays since the festivals took place during daytime under the hot Aegean sun. It is easy to understand why the Ancient Greeks personified the sun as a god (*Apollo*), since the beautiful sun and the clear blue water of the Greek Islands and surrounding coastal areas are a Mediterranean paradise.

Props/Machinery

Ancient Greek plays used various props and pieces of stage machinery. One mechanical device—called a *deus ex machina*—lifted up actors in a kind of aggrandizement or *apotheosis*. Characters could ascend to heaven by means of this elevator-style winch, and gods could sometimes descend to the real world with it.

Costumes

Costumes worn by the actors were stereotypical. Actors wore *chitons* (*togas*) and facemasks with generalized expressions on them. One theory says that they also wore elevator shoes (*kothorni*) lifting them anywhere from 6-8 inches off the ground so that their voices could be better heard in the theaters, and so that they could appear larger than life. The characters represented universal human types—the idea of a character, and not a specific actor—so they wore facemasks with either a smile or a frown to express universal human feelings.

ACTIVITY

Select a prop for a production of *Oedipus Rex*, do research on its origin and purpose, and then design a new version of the prop for an updated production of the play. Explain the reasoning behind your design.

SCRIPT/MUSIC

Script

The script was typically not a new story. Ancient Greeks went to the theater to see a story they knew well, not a new one. This contrasts sharply with audiences today who expect to see a new story every time they go to a movie theater (e.g., *Spiderman*® and its sequels). Ancient Greeks wanted to see a familiar story told in a new way—with new insight and variation—something like why people go to the *Great Passion Play* near Eureka Springs, Arkansas each year. Christian audience members know the story of Christ's *Passion*, but they want to see and hear a new performance of it. Stories in Ancient Greek dramas were derived from well-known myths, legends, and history. Desirable plots held up a flawed character as a hero and then metaphorically sacrificed him at the altar of the gods in order to restore world order.

Competitions for dramas were held during the spring at annual religious festivals such as the *Dionysia* in Athens. Performances consisted of two tragic dramas, two comedies, and a *satyr* play on the same day. *Satyr* plays are bawdy comedies based upon religious fertility rites where men dress up as huge human phalluses and chase each other around in a ridiculous fashion.

Music

One particular instrument was associated with the Ancient Greek tragedies: the *aulos* [pronounced: owl—awhs] has a noisy, inharmonic sound, and since terrible things happen in a tragedy, it is an appropriate instrument for the genre.

FIGURE 7.2 *Youth Playing the Aulos*, Detail of a Banquet Scene (Attic red-figure cup, ca. 460–450 B.C.E.), Euaion Painter. Louvre, Paris

Fine Art/Getty Images

Chorus

In addition to the *aulos*, the Greek chorus—a group of people who half-sing, half-speak words in meters appropriate to the action—commented upon the action. They moved from one side of the stage to another in choreography called *strophes* and *anti-strophes* that were as much stage directions as songs. The chorus comments upon the action, and fills in details about the background of the story. They are the mediators between the audience and the principal characters, and provide continuity throughout the drama.

PARTICIPANTS

Actors

Thespis, who delivered readings from a cart that he drove around from town to town, often gave solo readings in these theaters and occasionally had another actor who helped him. By 500 B.C.E., however, playwrights started to produce plays with three or four main actors, as well. The cast was male, even for the female roles.

Director

The director was typically the playwright himself, and the actors seconded as the stagehands and other helpers.

Choreographer

The choreographer was undoubtedly the director or someone with expertise in planning the arrangement of choral episodes on stage.

Audience

Not only did the general population attend these events, but prisoners were released from jail because it was thought that the plays were morally uplifting and would ultimately improve the conduct of those who saw them.

FINANCIAL SUPPORT

Producers

The scripts had to be reviewed and approved for production. In that sense, they were *Academy Award* winners of their time. The priest of the cult that met in the theater would be one of the judges. The theater was not just an auditorium, but a temple in a temple complex controlled by the priest of a cult who witnessed the ritual drama. In addition to support from the priest, the play would need financial support from a wealthy businessperson in town called the *choregus*—or producer.

Money

State funds were provided for the festival performances, since they reaffirmed life in the city-states of the time. Those who know the story of *Oedipus Rex*, for example, remember that the city of Thebes is saved at the end of the drama.

Publicity/Advertisements

Advertisements were unnecessary because audiences were ready-made. Everybody knew when the religious festivals took place each year and there was no admission charge for the poor.

Tickets

Since these festivals were state sponsored, everyone knew when the plays would occur and tickets were not necessary. Quite possibly spots were roped off for important visitors in the *theatron*, and parking lots were maintained for animal and cart storage for the day.

Programs

Programs as we know them were not necessary since everyone knew the stories of the plays, and quite possibly the actors and playwrights, too.

ELEMENTS OF DRAMA

Aristotle, celebrated student of Plato, produced two sets of writings entitled *On Poetry* and *Poetics*. *On Poetry* was available to Renaissance writers, but is now lost and only the *Poetics* remains. *Poetics* is an unfinished collection of writings on how one might construct a tragic play. According to Aristotle, a good tragic play requires plot, character, thought, diction, melody, and spectacle. Interestingly, these terms have now become the elements of drama. Thus, Aristotle is apparently the only person ever to have singularly invented the elements of an art form. Let us review the terms that Aristotle presents.

PLOT

Aristotle defines plot as the arrangement of the incidents in the story; he considered plot the most important.

CHARACTER

A good tragedy should show the moral qualities of people portrayed. Moral qualities have to do with good or bad choices. People have to make choices in this life—are the characters making good choices or bad ones in this drama?

THOUGHT

The drama ought to tell us something universal about people. It is not enough to produce a play about people; it should speak to us universally and enunciate general truths about life. A play should imitate life through the idea of *mimesis*.

DICTION

According to Aristotle, there are two ways to communicate with people in a drama. The meaning of the words can be delivered in prose (i.e., normal conversation) or in spoken verse (i.e., rhymed or repeating rhythms). Fixed meters were used to convey affect appropriate to the action in an Ancient Greek drama.

MELODY

Musical accompaniment in a tragedy is reserved principally for one instrument—the *aulos* (Figure **7.2**). The *aulos* is a double reed instrument with a very gross sound, and high noise content. It was also used in Ancient Greek warfare to set the tone of the battle.

SPECTACLE

Staging, costume, and machinery are important. However, Aristotle cautions against excessive use of these devices because they can hide a weakness in the script as a whole.

STRUCTURE OF PLOT

Aristotle took the first element, Plot, from the list above and subdivided it into several categories: Exposition/Prologue, Inciting Incident, Complication, Crisis, and Resolution. Bracketed items may have been added by later writers, since Aristotle's supplementary discussion to the *Poetics* is now lost.

[EXPOSITION/PROLOGUE]

Information about earlier events is presented. Actually, it summarizes information already known to the audience.

[INCITING INCIDENT]

The inciting incident establishes the conflict of the play.

COMPLICATION

Discoveries by characters change the course of their actions.

CRISIS

A turning point marks the fall of the hero from which there is no turning back.

RESOLUTION

The resolution ties together loose ends, brings the play to a close, and restores world order.

FORCES OF ACTION

In addition to the basic structure of plot, Aristotle mentions two other internal features that help propel the action forward: Recognition scenes and Reversals. Aristotle said that when a character recognizes the truth, this recognition may change the course of action. He also said that the best kind of play occurs when a Recognition Scene coincides with an unexpected outcome (Reversal).

OEDIPUS REX (WHO AM I?)

Oedipus: "Oh Zeus, what have you planned to do to me?"

Sophocles' play *Oedipus Rex* translates as *King Clubfoot* (*Oedipus* = clubfoot and *Rex* = King) and it was the runner up among competitors the year it was chosen (429 B.C.E.) among plays produced in Athens. Both the winner and the runner-up were typically produced each year, so it obviously impressed everyone even though it did not win the "Academy Award." In fact, it impressed the philosopher Aristotle so much that he cited it as an excellent example of tragedy in his *Poetics*.

Before reading or listening to the play, however, a spectator should know the background of the story in detail—just as the Ancient Greeks did who attended the festivals twenty-five centuries ago. Educated people who knew the story and its history were able to appreciate the drama on a higher level than those who were simply dropped down into the action without knowing what was is going on.

If you were to ask someone to summarize the plot of *Oedipus Rex* today, they might say "Oedipus killed his father, married his mother, and lived in incest with her—raising inbred children." This is the outline of the story, but so much is missing from this simplistic representation of the story that we are cheated of insight. As modern viewers, we have an obligation to know the background of the story in order to understand how such a horrific situation could take place. Let us pick up the threads of the legend, myth, and history surrounding the *Oedipus* story to find out how this situation developed.

OEDIPUS REX: BACKGROUND

People in Ancient Greece often said they could trace their ancestors back to gods such as *Apollo* or *Zeus*. Is it any wonder then that Oedipus' family could trace their origins back to the gods? The gods were psychological prototypes of human beings who argued among themselves just as people did, but also tried to resolve their disagreements by involving living men. A curse was placed on the whole line of Oedipus' family because of a dispute between the gods. Why some members of Oedipus' family escaped the curse is not explained, but the stories have come down as myth and legend preserved in plays such as Sophocles' *Oedipus Rex*. Let us go to a point in the story of the family where Oedipus' father, Laius, is a young man. Those who know even this much background to the story will be able to appreciate the total effect much better.

Laius was visiting Pelop's house (on the PELOPonnesus) and received the protection and hospitality of the home. In that time this was a special privilege; it meant more than simply receiving a free dinner and a place to stay for the night. The person also received protection from his enemies—even if they were in pursuit. While staying at Pelop's house, Laius fell in love with Pelop's son. It is not clear from the surviving stories whether he seduced Pelop's son or simply kidnapped him, but the two of them took off together. Pelops was so furious at the loss of his only son that he prayed to the Goddess of Households for vengeance. Pelop's prayers were heard, and the gods decided that Laius was a housebreaker who should be punished.

Evidently, Laius later became disinterested in Pelops' son because he subsequently married Jocaste. This young couple wanted to know what the future would hold for them, so they did what all good Greeks would do. They went to Delphi—the center of the Greek universe—to consult the Oracle. The Oracle was an elderly woman who sat at the mouth of a cave and "spoke in tongues"—possibly because of the sulfur fumes that spewed out of the mountain where she sat. Occasionally, she flew into fits that caused the eagles sitting on perches near her to scream. When she spoke, priests would translate her words into language that ordinary mortals could understand.

When the Oracle saw Laius, she started to speak in tongues, the eagles screamed, and the priests took dictation. They told Laius and Jocaste that the gods had decided to have Laius' first son kill him in retaliation for having broken up Pelop's house and that Laius' son would live in incest with his wife as punishment. In arrogance (*Hubris*), Laius decided to defy the gods and said "Oh no, you won't," and he resolved to kill his first-born son to prevent the curse. Laius and Jocaste returned to Thebes (north of Athens, Greece) where he was the headman, or leader of the town. When their first-born son arrived, Laius tied up the baby's ankles so tightly with leather straps and metals pieces that it caused permanent lameness. He gave the baby to a shepherd, and sent him up to Mount Citharon about 30 miles south of Thebes to kill the child, and get rid of the curse.

The shepherd, however, felt sorry for the baby and decided to give him to another shepherd from Corinth (located ironically in the *Peloponnesus*), about 60 miles south, on the other side of Mount Citharon. Since those were enormous distances at that time, Laius' shepherd thought no one would ever hear from the child again. The child was raised in the house of the king and queen at Corinth who were childless, Polybus and Merobe.

Life continued happily for all concerned. Laius and Jocaste were doing well in Thebes while Oedipus grew up in Corinth with his foster parents Polybus and Merobe. One day, however, a drunk yelled out in a party that Oedipus was not his father's son. Surprised to learn that he was an adopted child, Oedipus asked his parents about it, but they denied everything. Secretly, Oedipus went to the place where all good Greeks went to find out information—Delphi—to consult the Oracle.

When he arrived, the Delphic Oracle began to speak in tongues, the eagles screamed, and the priests took dictation. Oedipus asked what the future held for him. The priests told him that the gods had put a terrible curse on him: that he was going kill his father, live in incest with his mother and raise children that other people would shudder to see. Oedipus said, "Oh no, I won't." He too, had arrogance (*Hubris*). "I'm never going back to Corinth as long as I live. I will never see my parents Polybus and Merobe (really his step-parents) again." He decided to defy the gods and drove his chariot north from Delphi.

As he drove down the stone road near Dauhlia, where three roads meet, Oedipus saw another chariot coming very fast in the opposite direction. It appeared to belong to someone important because there were horses and riders in front of the vehicle. It was clear to Oedipus by the manner in which they were racing down the road that they were going to drive him off the road into a ditch. Unfortunately, Oedipus had a character flaw. Whenever he got mad he would blow up uncontrollably. These reckless roadsters made him so mad that he clubbed the driver of the chariot over the head as he passed by. An old man in the chariot responded by hitting Oedipus on the head with his cane. There was a collision, and the chariots dispersed across the road. Oedipus came back and killed all of them in a rage.

At the time, Oedipus didn't realize that the old man in the chariot was his real father, Laius. Laius was on his way to Delphi to find out what the gods wanted to end a plague currently affecting Thebes. His death temporarily satisfied them.

Oedipus continued his journey and arrived at Thebes where a sphinx was sitting at the city gate. The sphinx, responsible for a putrefied water supply, bad crops and other problems would not leave until someone could answer his question: "What walks on fours in the early part of life, on twos in the middle of life, and on threes in the evening of life." Clever Oedipus answered the question correctly, "It is man—who crawls on all fours as a baby (in the morning of his life), walks on two legs, erect (in the afternoon of his life) and uses a cane to walk on three legs (in the evening of his life)." The sphinx was satisfied and disappeared. Oedipus became the town hero, the plagues went away, the water cleared up, and crops started to grow. The gods seemed to be satisfied and everyone was again happy.

In the meantime, the citizens of Thebes learned that Laius (Oedipus' father) had been killed in a road accident. Since they did not have a headman anymore, they decided to make Oedipus their headman. Why not take the hero who had just set the town free of a sphinx to be the headman?

In those days, the headman told everyone what to do and how to think. Oedipus inherited the palace, buildings, animals and other property owned by Laius. Women were property, so Oedipus inherited Jocaste (not knowing she was his mother) and took her for his own wife. They lived together and raised children who had a peculiar look about them due to the inbreeding. (This is often shown by distorted features on the facemasks worn by actors in Ancient Greek plays.)

All of the information above would have been known to an educated audience of Ancient Greeks and would have influenced their reaction to the dramatic tragedy.

STRUCTURE OF PLOT IN *OEDIPUS*

1. **EXPOSITION/PROLOGUE:** The announcer tells us that there is a curse on the family, the oracle has predicted disaster, and Thebes is having a new plague.

2. **INCITING INCIDENT:** No one seems to know what is the cause of the problem. Oedipus, as headman, is trying to figure out who or what is causing this disaster, and how the problem can be solved. His brother-in-law Kreon tells him to send for an old blind philosopher named Tyresius who informs Oedipus that HE is the problem. Oedipus thinks that Kreon has hatched a plot to remove him from his job as headman and does not believe the old philosopher—who cannot see anyway.

3. **COMPLICATION:** Oedipus' question is converted into another question "Who Am I?" As Oedipus attempts to figure out who is responsible for the plague, he [and the people around him] starts to realize that perhaps HE is the problem. These are called recognition scenes, and Aristotle says they drive the action forward as characters learn the truth.

4. **CRISIS:** At the crisis of the play, Oedipus discovers that indeed HE is the problem, the bad apple, or the disease of Thebes. He is the person who must be carved out of society. He has to be sacrificed at the theatrical altar in order to satisfy the gods. Aristotle says *Oedipus Rex* illustrates tragedies best because a major Reversal coincides with the crisis. In a Reversal, an action that is expected to have one result produces exactly the opposite. Oedipus thinks that by questioning everybody he will learn who is at fault and thereby set himself and Thebes free. Oedipus is surprised to learn that he is the problem, that he is the one with whom the gods are upset, and that he is the one who must be removed from society to restore world order. This cleansing is referred to by Aristotle as *Catharsis*.

5. **RESOLUTION:** Oedipus rushes into his wife's/mother's bedroom where she has committed suicide. In a rage, he pokes out his own eyes with a broach from her dress. Oedipus ends up blinded and destroyed—exactly the things predicted by the blind philosopher Tyresius early in the play.

With this background information you are in a position to appreciate the complete play by Sophocles. However, it is important to note that Sophocles made his own artistic contribution to the story by lacing it with ironic references to the characters. His version of the story play is riddled with ironic references to seeing, sight, revelation, knowing, and recognizing. Oedipus tries to find out who or what is at fault for the problems in Thebes, and makes repeated references to seeing, sight, and sunlight ("It's as clear as sunlight to me now."). He does not realize that Zeus (head of the gods), has appointed Apollo (the sun god) to bring his downfall. At one point, Oedipus exclaims, "Perhaps the old blind man (Tyresius) can actually see…." and toward the end of the play he says, "it's as clear as sunlight now." When Jocaste discovers who Oedipus is, she exclaims "May the gods prevent you from the knowledge of who you are." She then runs offstage to commit suicide—falling into permanent blindness. When Oedipus sees Jocate's hanging body, he grabs the broach from her dress and stabs his own eyes, also falling into permanent blindness.

A convenient point at which to begin reading falls at the beginning of Act II. A messenger from Corinth shows up in Thebes to tell Oedipus that he is the new king of Corinth. But Oedipus does not want to go back to his stepparents' home for fear of the prophesies told by the Delphic oracle. The messenger tells him his fears are groundless, but Oedipus does not realize that they are not his real parents. He was found on Mount Citharon and saved from death by this very messenger who got him from a shepherd. Oedipus asks to hear the story directly from the shepherd. Jocaste realizes (recognition scene) what has happened and tells him not to go further with the investigation. Persistent, however, Oedipus interrogates the old shepherd and learns the truth about who he really is. At this point there is a major reversal at the crisis of the play. Oedipus learns that he is the problem; that he is the person who has angered the gods and that he is the one who has to be removed from society in order for world order to be restored.

CHAPTER 7

You should now view the play. Many translations and performances of Oedipus Rex are available online.

CATHARSIS: A MEDICAL-RELIGIOUS RITUAL

Cleansing, washing, and bathing were basic rituals at the Ancient Greek temples. The cleansing and purification process was extended to the psychological level in Ancient Greek Theater. A visitor coming to a temple complex such as Delphi might visit a number of places seeking help from the gods for a physical ailment before going to the theater. S/he would give offerings, wash, and bathe. Sometimes prayers alone were enough to get results. In severe cases, medicine was practiced by the priests. One of the most potent forms of medical healing was the use of snakes—either the use of snake venom or the laying of snakes upon the sick person. People were willing to undergo whatever medical practices prevailed at the time in order to have their physical ailments resolved. One can see the various tools that were used for medical operations (even brain surgery) in the museums today at the temple complexes of Delphi or Olympia.

The Ancient Greek theater was an extension of the physical healing process. It contained an altar for the slaughter of animal sacrifices. Over time, the sacrifices were stylized into a psychological slaughter of a human character in a play such as *Oedipus Rex*. Because the gods were upset with Oedipus, he had to be removed from society in order for world order to be restored.

As a psychological parallel to physical disorder, the removing of Oedipus and restoring of Thebes was comparable to removing poisons from and restoring the body. In essence, an attendee at the Ancient Greek theater was undergoing a psychological purification or treatment parallel to the physical cures offered elsewhere in the temple complex. This psychological cleansing is known as *Catharsis* or purification.

A visitor to the temple complex might work his/her way among the sacred buildings, receiving physical and spiritual treatment in buildings we might now refer to as the Department of Oncology, the Department of Surgery, or the Department of Pediatrics. The theater might be thought of as the Department of Psychiatry—offering psychological cleansing (*Catharsis*).

The Oedipus legend is so famous in the history of theater and intellectual thought that Sigmund Freud labeled one of his emotional disorders after the story that resulted in a popular thumbnail version of the tale in which a man has an attachment to his mother. The acts portrayed in Oedipus Rex are highly prohibitive. Not only are they repulsive acts, but society has strong admonitions against them. Genetic inbreeding is strongly condemned by the state. It is perhaps no accident that the Oedipus story has been used for psychological diagnoses, because it was used to promote psychological *Catharsis* (purification) in the original Ancient Greek temples.

Please suggest a design for a new production of *Oedipus Rex*. You should select a theme or an era to represent (possibilities might include the 1960s, 1970s, or 1980s). Do research on the theme or time period and collect images into a collage to ensure consistent application of the theme to costumes and staging. Decide what personality archetypes are represented in this play and design costumes and face masks appropriate for each character. Then, go through the elements of design for each character and decide how the costume and face mask should look in terms of color and texture. You should end up with a remarkably creative departure from the original productions seen by Ancient Greek audiences.

CRITICAL METHOD APPLICATION

Apply the Critical Method to Sophocles' work, *Oedipus Rex*. Remember, as discussed in Chapter One, the steps include Description, Analysis, Interpretation, and Evaluation.

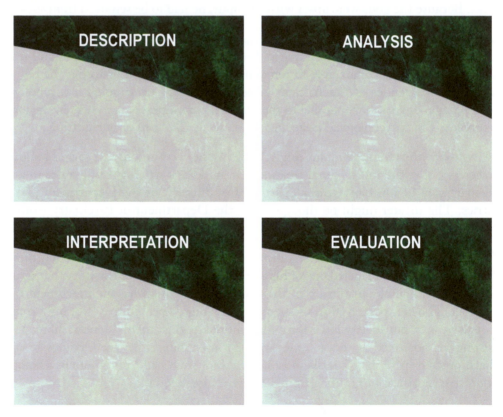

DESCRIPTION

ANALYSIS

INTERPRETATION

EVALUATION

CRITICAL TERMS

ELEMENTS OF TRAGEDY

PLOT	Arrangement of incidents; complication/unraveling
CHARACTER	Moral qualities of people portrayed
THOUGHT	Enunciation of general truths (mimesis)
DICTION	Expression of meaning in words (prose/verse)
MELODY	Musical accompaniment
SPECTACLE	Staging; Costumes; Machinery

ELEMENTS OF PLOT

COMPLICATION	Discoveries that change the course of the action
CRISIS	Turning point
EXPOSITION/ PROLOGUE	Information about earlier events is presented
INCITING INCIDENT	Establishes the conflict
RESOLUTION	Ties together loose ends

ADDITIONAL TERMS

REVERSAL	An action expected to have one result, produces the opposite
RECOGNITION SCENE	Character learns the truth

REVIEW QUESTION

Which of the following is Oedipus' "Fatal Flaw?"

1. Catharsis
2. Hubris
3. Entasis
4. Crisis
5. Synopsis

Answer spelled backwards: sirbuh.

CRITICAL COMMENTARY

Drama presents issues of choice, consequence, and conduct that are perennial in life and business; it is useful to understand them in order to know what promotes good commerce and business relations. Oedipus' fatal flaw may be described as both his arrogance (*Hubris*) and his tendency to blow up. The important critical lesson about him is that he represents a universal archetype of human psychology.

Tragic drama shows that some stories can clearly improve people, if not physically as the temple priests might have hoped for, then at least morally. Tragic plays are about improving psychological conduct and they share parallels with medical rituals that attempt to improve physical comportment.

DANCE
A COMPOUND ART FORM

"Dance is music made visible."
—George Balanchine (1904–1983)

INTRODUCTION

Dance is the art of the human figure in motion—assuming positions, executing moves, designing patterns, and making gestures—usually to the accompaniment of music and spectacle (costumes, staging, etc.). Thus, it is essentially a compound art form. Dance can be improvisatory or highly regulated with prescribed formal movements and choreography. It may exploit the possibilities of the human mechanism in order to amaze the spectator (as in the Brazilian *Capoeira* that combines dance and martial arts), it can celebrate a bountiful harvest (rainmaking and religious dances), or it can provide entertainment (as in breakdancing, Figure **8.1**). The three types of dance are Ritual, Narrative, and Absolute.

FIGURE 8.1 Breakdance

TYPES OF DANCE

RITUAL/HEALING

From the dawn of time, people have used dance in religious ceremonies. Many of these dances involved healing or attempts to dispel evil spirits. Some were designed to bring a person into religious ecstasy as a kind of sedative to illness, or to worship spirits in the hope that they would bring a good harvest. Dance rituals celebrate events as diverse as birth, the coming of age, and marriage (Figure **8.2**). Sometimes dance is intended as a simple emotional release as in Ancient Greek *Bacchae* orgies, where drunken dancers work themselves in to a frenzy of excitement.

FIGURE 8.2 African Tribal Dance

NARRATIVE

Dances often incorporate themes and story lines enhanced by the geometry of movement. This is particularly true of 19th century dance that brought a special emphasis to the dance narrative with extensive pantomime (movement that mimics speech gestures), traditional steps, and choreography. Typically, the stories of 19th century ballets, like operas of the period, involve frustrated love compounded by the unpredictability of the supernatural—with scenes set at night in order to take advantage of the newly gas-lit theaters. Men dominated the dance stage in earlier eras, whereas the female ballerina wearing a *tutu* (Figure **8.3**) dominated 19th century ballet in stories about frustrated love.

FIGURE 8.3 Swan *Lake*, music by Pyotr Ilyich Tchaikovsky, Russian National Ballet (October 2, 2010). Jincheng Art Theater, Chengdu, China

ABSOLUTE

Absolute dance does not require a narrative. *Les Sylphides* (not to be confused with an earlier ballet, *La Sylphide)* is a good example of this dance type (Figure **8.4**). Freed from the narrative, it is a pivotal work leading into the abstract dance styles of the 20th century. While numerous dance styles have evolved from the sense of freedom engendered by 20th century culture, perhaps the most interesting dance movements are the improvised styles based upon "chance operations," as in the performances of Merce Cunningham. The freedom from traditional ballet fixed steps has created new forms of dance where the movements of audience members themselves create patterns in space.

FIGURE 8.4 Mika Yoshioka and Vladimir Malakhov dance the ouverture 'Les Sylphides' during rehearsal of 'Malakhov & Friends The Final"

ELEMENTS OF DANCE

There is no general agreement about the exact number of elements in the art of dance. Some writers suggest three elements and others suggest more. A general list is given below:

1. **BODY.** The body can create numerous shapes or designs in space.
2. **ACTION/MOVEMENT.** The body can crouch, jump, reach, step, crawl, bend, and twist; each of these positions helps define shapes in space.
3. **SPACE.** Space includes both the location of the performance (on stage or out-of-doors) and the perimeter of the dancer's movements.
4. **TIME.** The rate at which a dancer's steps or positions change—either fast or slow; changes are usually organized around musical pulse beats.
5. **ATTACK/ENERGY.** Movements can begin aggressively or with caution; turns can be taken slowly or quickly.
6. **CHOREOGRAPHY.** A general pattern of motion can result from the combination of movements or steps.
7. **SPECTACLE.** This element involves music, staging, costumes, and so forth that support the dance.

BALLET

Ballet is a type of dance where the motion of the human body and its choreography take precedence over other artistic elements. Costumes are prescribed, staging is often limited, steps are fixed, and gestures come from established traditions. Dancers usually engage in moves that are counterparts to the musical sounds, even if they do not simply follow the beat of the music. If a melodic turn occurs in the music, the dancers often move their head, arms, legs, and body to interpret that sound.

Ballet tradition extends back to the court of Catherine de Medici in the 16th century when choreographer Balthazar de Beaujoyeaulx produced a five and one-half hour spectacle entitled *Ballet comique de la reine* (1581). Considered one of the first ballets, this production combined comedy with people dancing in geometrical patterns. Courtiers performed in these spectacles in order to see and be seen in fashionable costumes at court.

During the Renaissance, pairs of dances such as the *Pavane* and *Galliarde* provided recreation and entertainment at wealthy court gatherings. Couples lined up in rows, both in open (standing apart) and close (paired together) position—facing each other (mirroring) or moving in lines across the floor space following each other (canon). On several occasions ladies and gentlemen were wheeled into large festival halls on floats and descended to the floor in elaborate dance spectacles. The popularity of these choreographed Italian pageants spread to courts throughout Europe.

Skilled in the art of dance, Louis XIV established academies in France that led to the development of professional dance—with elaborate, themes, music, spectacle, and precise moves for the dancers. The king himself appeared in numerous productions at the palaces of the Louvre and Versailles. His court entertainments developed into what eventually became professional ballet at the *Académie Royale de Danse* in 1661. The academy established standards for the art of dance and accredited dance instructors. Ballet steps were reduced to formulas such as *plié, demi plié,* and *grand plié* (a type of double knee bend) that could be choreographed into stage spectacles.

Jean Baptiste Lully, composer to Louis XIV, directed the *Académie Royale de Musique* that included the Paris Opera Ballet—the first professional ballet company. Many French terms associated with dance steps come from this early dance organization; it is still functioning today as the Paris Opera and its style is influential throughout the world. The first director of the *Académie Royale de Danse*, Pierre Beauchamp, created his own system for recording the dance steps and is now credited with inventing the five basic positions of the feet shown in Figures **8.5–8.9**.

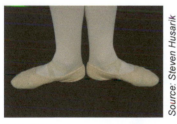
Source: Steven Husarik

FIGURE 8.5 First position

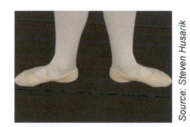
Source: Steven Husarik

FIGURE 8.6 Second position

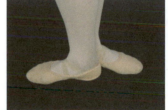
Source: Steven Husarik

FIGURE 8.7 Third position

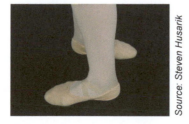
Source: Steven Husarik

FIGURE 8.8 Fourth position

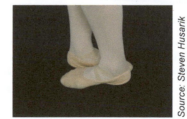
Source: Steven Husarik

FIGURE 8.9 Fifth position

Numerous additional body positions associated with dance were codified over the years. For example, there are the positions of the arms (*Porte de bras*) that vary in number with each school of ballet. Other key movements include turns (*pirouette*), leaps (*jeté*), or leg kicks (*battement*). Each of these moves (figures) can be combined with others to create a choreographic display. Since most of them come from the French Academy, they are typically designated with French labels.

ACTIVITY

Imagine that you are holding a basketball ball in your hands. Maneuver the ball in different directions. Pass it by your chest, pass it over your head, pass it behind your back, and pass it between your legs. Now, hand the imaginary ball to someone else. As you complete each move you are engaging in arm movements that are the modern equivalents of *Porte de bras*.

Nineteenth century ballets combined dance with professional dancers, narratives, costumes, staging, troupes of dancers, pantomime, and mixtures of traditional dance with courtly steps. In a classic example of art imitating art, celebrated 19th century dance theoretician Carlo Blasis (1797–1878) invented the step called "Attitude" by deriving it from a statue of *Mercury* by Giovanni Bologna. (Figure **8.10** and Figure **8.11**).

Vincenzo Fontana/Getty Images

AYakovlev/Shutterstock.com.

ostill/Shutterstock.com.

FIGURE 8.10 Mercury (1580), Jean Boulogne, incorrectly known as Giovanni da Bologna (ca. 1524–1608), bronze, 180 cm, Bargello, Florence, inspired the ballet step "Attitude."

FIGURE 8.11 Ballerina with classical-style tutu in pose of "Attitude" (lifted leg is bent at 90-degree angle)

FIGURE 8.12 Ballerina with classic tutu in pose of "Arabesque" (lifted leg is straight). Ostill

Ballet steps are often similar to one another and can be easily confused. For example, "Attitude" is very similar to "Arabesque," except that in "Attitude" the lifted leg is turned at a 90–degree angle (as in the statue from which it derives), while "Arabesque" has the lifted leg extended in a straight line (Figure **8.12**). The starting position, movement, and completion of each step forms a sequence of motions that cannot easily be captured in a single photographic shot.

One of the most visually distinctive ballet steps, *Fouetté en tournant* (whipped by turning), consists of a dancer repeatedly rising from the flat foot to toe on one leg, completing a full turn, and then returning to flat foot position—all of this is accomplished by propelling the action with the whipping leg. A striking example occurs in the coda to the *pas de deux* of *Swan Lake* (music by Pyotr IlyichTchaikovsky) where the dancer must perform thirty-two turns in a row.

Choreology is the study, description, and analysis of dance movements, while the art of arranging the steps or movements into sequences and patterns is called choreography. Choreography derives from the Ancient Greek words "circle dance-writing" and refers to the organized placement of dancers and choristers in the theaters of Ancient Greece. It was 20th century choreographer, George Balanchine, who actually coined the term. With a vocabulary of steps and positions, the choreographer is free to design movement in space and relate figures to one another almost in the way a film director/editor arranges and combines scenes and shots in a film. Movement of the dancer(s) across the stage, streamlining hand gestures, raising and lowering of the arms, positioning the feet in basic position, and engaging in turns are all parts of this kinetic art form.

STANDING *EN POINTE*

One of the unique features of 19th century ballet is that female dancers rise up on their toes, *en pointe*. Charles Didelot (1767–1837) developed a device with wires to make ballerinas appear as if they were flying or standing on their toes (*en pointe*). Eventually, special ballet shoes were developed to enable dancers to stand *en pointe* without wires. A box wrapped under the toes in the ballet slipper that supported the foot enabled the dancer not only to rise up upon the toes, but even to achieve great leaps and return to the *en pointe* position. This skill was a metaphor for art and science of the 19th century that continually speculated on ways to fly.

ACTIVITY

Please select your favorite song and choreograph it with various steps of your own choosing. It may be useful to create a "theme" or story to match the song and the steps. Decide whether you want one or more people to perform the dance. Then, improvise some steps that follow the beat of the music and select the best ones for a cell phone recording.

CRITICAL METHOD APPLICATION

Apply the Critical Method to Tchaikovsky's work, *Swan Lake*. You may view any reputable dance company's video recording of *Swan Lake*. Remember, as discussed in Chapter One, the steps include Description, Analysis, Interpretation, and Evaluation.

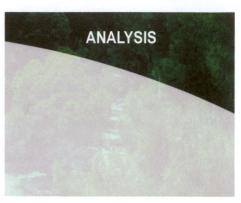

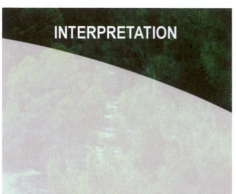

TYPES OF DANCE

RITUAL/HEALING	Dances that involved attempts at healing or catharsis
NARRATIVE	Dances that incorporate themes or story lines
ABSOLUTE	Dances that have no story

DANCE ELEMENTS

BODY	Body parts can create shapes or designs in space
MOVEMENT	Body positions can define shapes in space
STEP	Basic three-part action
ATTACK	Beginning of a step
SPACE	Perimeter of the dancer's movements
TIME	Rate at which moves change
CHOREOGRAPHY	Steps can be organized into meaningful patterns
ROUTINE	A series of dance steps
SPECTACLE	Music, projections, and staging that support the dance

ADDITIONAL TERMS

ARABESQUE	Standing *en pointe*, the lifted leg is straight
ATTITUDE	Standing *en pointe*, the lifted leg is turned at a 90-degree angle
CHASSÉ	One foot moves forward and the other follows or "chases" it
DEMI- PLIÉ	Half knee bend
DÉVELOPÉ	Draw one leg up, foot touches supporting leg, and then extends
EN POINTE	Dancer supports body weight on the tips of toes
GRAND PLIÉ	Bend to the deepest position
JETÉ	Jump from one foot to another that throws the dancer a distance
MISE EN SCÈNE	Stage design
PANTOMIME	Movement that mimics speech gestures
PAS DE BOURREÉ COURU	Running on toe tips
PIROUETTE	Controlled whirl or spin from Plié to Relevé
PLIÉ	Moving up and down with a continuous bending of the knees
RELEVÉ	Rising to full position on the toes
ROND DE JAMB	Circular movement of the leg
TENDU	One leg is stretched out—sometimes a few inches above floor

The ballet step where a dancer rises from the flat foot to extended position (*en pointe*) while doing a full turn and then returning to flat foot position is called:

1. Mise en scene (staging)
2. Demi-plie (half fold)
3. Arabesque
4. Fouetté en tournant (whipped by turning)
5. Ronds de jambs a terre.

Only one answer applies—all others are incorrect.

(Answer spelled backwards: tnanruot ne etteuof)

CRITICAL COMMENTARY

Dance criticism and commentary is an open venue for the average person in our age because of the Internet. It is now possible to evaluate, share opinions, and see productions online that were previously discussed only by a limited number of connoisseurs. With an increased size of the critical audience, dance is evaluated from a greater number of perspectives. Thus, dance now engages discussions over both theories of ballet (requiring a knowledge of choreographic design), and sports and acrobatics (requiring a knowledge mechanical maneuverability).

FILM
A COMPOUND ART FORM

*"Failure is unimportant. It takes courage
to make a fool of yourself."*
—Charlie Chaplin (1889–1977)

INTRODUCTION

Perhaps more than any other art form, film has emerged as the result of achievements in the fields of science and technology. Countless film pioneers such as Eadweard Muybridge (1830–1904) and Étienne-Jules Marey (1830–1904) were more focused on scientific study than artistic product—even though their early products gave rise to the imagination of dramatic films in others. Max Skladanowsky (1863–1939) in Germany, George Méliès (1861–1938) and the Lumière brothers in France, and Thomas Edison (1847–1931) in America all added to the growth of this medium.

The circumstance of the United States as a leader in film was attributable in large part to the transference of New Yew York studios to southern California. This practical relocation to the sunny clime of California allowed producers to film outdoors the entire year. The new location gave Hollywood an economic advantage over studios in Europe because indoor shots required electric arc lamps costing as much as 300 dollars apiece (Figure **9.1**) were no longer absolute necessities in the sunlight of California.

FIGURE 9.1 Left to right: Arro Lights Cast-Iron Stage Light

Over the years, the film industry has refined the art form by adopting and inventing technologies such as 3D (1915), advanced color film (1935), surround sound (1939), *Cinerama* (1939), wide screen (1950), digital sound (1967), *IMAX* (1967), sound synchronization (1969), steady cam (1975), stadium seating (1976), digital projection (1992), and numerous other technical advances. With the invention of digital film and sound, almost every aspect of the industry has changed.

Since so much has already been written about film narratives, this chapter focuses almost exclusively upon two neglected aspects of film criticism: editing/camera techniques and musical sound.

TYPES OF FILM

NARRATIVE

Narrative film tells a story and is the most popular form of this medium. Since stories carry the action and sustain interest, the whole history of film is linked to narrative films. Even early silent films included narrative subtitles. Perhaps the most important development in narrative films came from George Méliès who used the technique of jump cuts to accomplish visual tricks on screen. Later directors applied the jump cut technique to explain action from various points of view—even in parallel story development—thus giving audiences an almost superhuman knowledge as events unfold in the narrative. Celebrated examples of narrative films include *Bridge on the River Kwai* (1957), *Casablanca* (1942), *and Lawrence of Arabia* (1962).

DOCUMENTARY

Documentary films record actuality. A long tradition of film making beginning with Edison's first recorded images, and the Lumière brothers' recordings of Paris, has resulted in magnificent documentary films today. Many of these show life at a particular time, place, or setting; others have a political motivation. *Triumph of the Will*, a Nazi-party film (1935) from Nuremburg, showed the political struggle in Germany before World War II. *Night and Fog* (1955), on the other hand, showed the horrific consequences of that struggle and its aftermath following the same war. Many successful documentary TV series have been produced over the years including the retrospective World War II series *Victory at Sea* (1952-1953) and its more recent counterpart *Wings of the Luftwaffe* (1993). Some current examples include medical documentaries such as *Trauma in the E.R.*, or wildlife films such as the *National Geographic Explorer* and the *Jacques Costeau Series* (1868-1976). The most artistically successful documentaries such as *The Fires of Kuwait* (1992) or *The Space Shuttle Series* (at Kennedy Space Center, Florida) have come from the *IMAX* series presented in large, specially-designed theaters that explore nature and history with high resolution cinematography and surround sound.

EXPERIMENTAL

Experimental films exist for their own sake and usually have a very limited story line or none at all. This type of film quickly tires the viewer because it emphasizes editing, camera angles, and sometimes sound that alone cannot carry the weight of a film. Experimental films are most effective in short TV commercials—especially those intended to appeal to a youth market—where they quickly catch the viewer's attention for a sales pitch. Images seen through water or smoked glass, or sounds speeded up or slowed down, quickly catch the viewer's attention but also quickly lose it without a narrative. The grandest example of experimental film with no overall story is Walt Disney's (1901-1966) *Fantasia* (1939).

ELEMENTS OF FILM

1. PLOT

Traditionally, critics discuss films in terms of their plots, characterization, and acting. Please see Chapter 16 for examples of two 20th-century films analyzed in this manner. Analysis of the structure of plot is a reasonable starting point for film criticism, but it is often emphasized at the expense of two other equally important aspects of this compound art form. As much as anything else, film is about moving images—camera and editing techniques—and soundtrack/music, which carries the emotion.

2. FILM TECHNIQUES

The basic unit of film-making is the shot, which includes camera angles, editing, lighting, set, timing, and so forth. It includes not only a still image of the action at any point, but also how action proceeds across a multiplicity of images (as illustrated in storyboards). Organizing shots into a point of view is the domain of the director, camera operator, and editor. Each sequence or scene is a building block in the action that is edited with film techniques. Certainly it is not imperative for one to be able to define an editor's term such as "wipe line" in order to discuss a film, but the viewer should appreciate that wipe lines can help organize the action of the film and sometimes function like the turning of a page in a comic book. For example, wipe lines combine with jump cuts help separate scenes of two opposing forces—the Empire and the Rebels—in a film such as Star Wars (1977–2005). A combination of film techniques strengthens the parallel story development of the film.

3. SOUND

Despite the fact that music carries the weight of the emotion in a film, it is frequently avoided in film criticism. Nearly the entire soundtrack of the movie *Platoon* (1986) is based upon a heart-rending piece of music by Samuel Barber entitled *Adagio for Strings*. Yet few critics of this film analyze the music or show its impact upon the film as a whole. Barber's original orchestral music unfolds over ten minutes, steadily grows to its climax, and then falls off to a resolution. In the film, however, Barber's music is cut into segments that are distributed across the drama. One of the most poignant musical segments occurs during the "village burning scene" and again at the end of the film where a helicopter pulls away from the jungle leaving the main character stranded among enemy soldiers. As an observer you may notice that the music gets steadily higher and louder (dynamic curve) at these climactic moments in the film. Nothing is said during these scenes because music, with its power to evoke feelings, expresses emotion to a degree that words cannot achieve. When music becomes an actor in this manner it is said to be *diegetic* (musical *diegesis*).

ACTIVITY

Please create a quick murder mystery (10 minutes in length) with story and dialog. Student-actors should form groups of six and improvise the story.

> The setting is a dark and stormy night, in a castle-like dark mansion on a hill. Thunder, rain, and the crack of lightning are heard in the background. Five people are being interviewed by a detective in a drawing room full of overstuffed couches with big armchairs and throw pillows.

> A rich old man who does not like any of his relatives and does not want to leave his money to them has been killed. Who did it? The stock characters are all dysfunctional types such as the spoiled rich daughter, the clueless rich son, a pompous butler, a shy maid, a blustery business associate who thinks he deserves an inheritance, and a wise detective.

Please show infighting among the suspects, how and why they might have killed the old man. Illustrate how the wise detective solves the problem.

If possible, engage in some character development (e.g., "You had more to gain from killing him than I did." "He hated me less than he hated you," etc.) and use some traditional elements of exposition, such as rising action, climax, etc. to define points where important aspects of plot occur.

FILM TECHNIQUES

The earliest films were simple affairs based upon the one camera shot. As the art form developed, however, camera movements and editing techniques quickly became a part of film-making and revolutionized it as an art form. Concepts such as pan, cant, and tilt (Figure **9.2**) became the first tools of film-makers, as well as those of the film critics. These critical terms are analogous to the tools used by tradespeople in their shops—both are useful only when applied to an appropriate situation. Twenty film techniques are given below in order to acquaint the reader with the critical tools of this trade. Please go to the film clips file online to see those techniques marked with a film reel. Explanations of each film technique are explained below in the context of famous films or television programs.

Camera

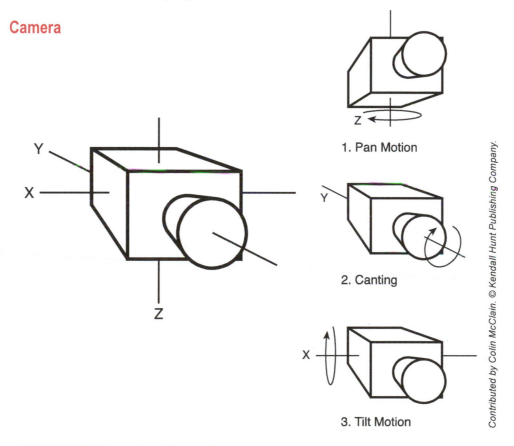

1. Pan Motion

2. Canting

3. Tilt Motion

FIGURE 9.2 Three Basic Camera Movements

▶ **1. PAN** (camera moves left or right). Pan motion occurs when a camera rotates from left to right on its Z axis (as shown in the diagram). People often use this technique when taking home movies. Ordinarily, panning involves movement just a few degrees to the right or left, however, the camera can be moved in (360 degrees) circles if desired. In *Saturday Night Fever* (1977), John Travolta dances in circles with his girlfriend and the camera is alternately substituted for each of the dance partners. The viewer sees each dancer holding onto the camera with hair flying in the wind as the camera turns (pans). The same pan technique occurs in one of the dance scenes in *Titanic* and is also used in shots involving 360-degree ("vrml") camera movements.

▶ **2. CANT** (camera rotates on its lens axis). Canting motion occurs whenever the camera is rotated upside down on the axis going through the lens (Y axis in the diagram). If the camera operator followed the motion of the camera s/he would literally turn upside down. A good example occurs in *Iron Eagle* (1986) and *Top Gun* (1986) where the camera is strapped to a plane that turns upside down in flight.

▶ **3. TILT** (camera moves up or down). Tilt motion occurs when the camera is rotated on its X axis (as shown in the diagram). This technique is often used to photograph skyscrapers—where the camera begins at ground level and tilts up to the top floor. It can give an impression of great height and scale.

▶ **4. ONE CAMERA SHOT** (fixed camera). Television programs that have a very important message, such as the *CNN* news broadcast, or the *Emergency Broadcast Channel*, lock the camera in one position. The dialog of a film must be compelling for this technique to be successful. A one camera shot occurs in a scene from the film *Clerks* (1994), where a girl seeks advice on a film rental. Although the scene lasts an entire minute with no camera movement, it succeeds because of the humorous conversation between the two actors.

5. EYE LEVEL CAMERA ANGLE (actor's eye level). A good example of this camera technique occurs in the "Cantina Scene" of *Star Wars*, where Luke and Obi-wan are sitting at a table with Han Solo while negotiating the rental of a space ship. The camera is placed so that the viewer is at eye level with the people sitting around the table—almost as if we, the viewers, are engaged in a conversation with Chewbacca, Han Solo, and Obi-Wan.

▶ **6. SLANTED OR ANGLE SHOTS** (view from above, side or below). These camera angles are often found in horror films such as *Dracula* (1931), or in *Jurassic Park* (1993) where the camera is located beneath the children in the front seat of the car while a huge *Tyrannosaurus rex* terrorizes them. Darth Vader is often seen at strange angles in *Star Wars* in order to stress his monstrous qualities.

7. DEPTH FOCUS (objects in foreground and background are in focus). In this method of focusing the camera, everything in the shot is crystal clear and in focus—every blade of grass in the foreground and every mountain in the distant landscape. Battle scenes of space ships in outer space typically use depth focus.

▶ **8. RACK FOCUS** (either foreground or background is focused). In contrast to depth focus, rack focus places objects in the foreground or background in focus, but not both. Usually an object in the foreground is shown slipping out of focus into some other object in the background. In *Arachnophobia* (1990)—a story about spiders—two young girls sing the song "the itsy bitsy spider crawls up the water spout" while the camera shifts out of focus from them to a spider climbing up a string just above their heads.

▶ **9. DOLLY (ZOOM)** Before the days of zoom lens, Hollywood technicians literally pulled the camera toward or away from an object in order to create the zoom effect. The camera was mounted on a truck with wheels called a "dolly," and the technique became known as dolly motion—a term that persists today. Modern viewers know the effect through movies such as *Wayne's World* (1992), where the image moves quickly in and out (zoom)—dolly motion to the extreme.

10. TRACK MOTION (camera mounted on a track). When a camera is mounted on a (railroad) track, it can follow the action while still maintaining a steady image. One of the best uses of this technique occurs during ESPN swimming meets. As the swimmers swim back and forth across the pool, a camera mounted on a track next to the pool easily follows the athletes back and forth.

▶ **11. TRUCK MOTION** (camera is mounted on a truck). Truck motion is useful to film herds of animals running in any direction across the plains. The movie *Twister* (1996), about chasing tornados, was a perfect venue for truck motion.

12. BOOM MOUNT (camera is located on a boom—usually attached to a truck). This is one of most common techniques for filming scenes. A good example would come from *Gone with the Wind* (1939) as the camera is lowered into the battlefield action.

13. IRIS IN/OUT (circle closes or opens). A favorite technique in early black and white silent films is often seen at the end of Warner Brothers' cartoons—a circle closes into a dot on a black screen.

14. HAND HELD CAMERA TECHNIQUE This film technique emulates the effect of someone walking around while holding a camera. Jarring bumps and turns in the image seem to knock the viewer one way or another. Sometimes the technique is used when the camera is not actually held by a cameraman—as in the *Jason Bourne* series (2002–2012) where the camera (on a wire) follows Bourne as he jumps from one building to another. Hand held camera technique places the viewer in the center of the action.

Film Editing

15. WIPE LINES (erase one image with another). This editing technique involves the insertion of a moving line that erases one image with another. The technique is found in *Star Wars* and various comic-book style film cartoons.

▶ **16. JUMPCUT** (immediate change to new scene or point of view). Perhaps the most powerful technique of film editing, a jump cut enables the film-maker to leap ahead or flash back in time in order to leave out unnecessary details. This technique helps propel the action of the film forward, and perhaps more than any other film technique adds to the superiority of the viewer's knowledge.

Imagine a scenario where a man kisses his girlfriend good-bye in Chicago and gets on a plane for Paris. After a jump cut, he gets off the plane and greets another girl with a kiss in Paris. The plot thickens! We gain superiority because we see things that the characters in the film may not see or know about, and the jump cut saves us a nine-hour jet flight from Chicago to Paris.

17. FORMCUT (overlap objects to connect two scenes). In Alfred Hitchcock's *Psycho* (1960), Marion (Janet Leigh) has been killed and is lying dead across the edge of the bathtub. The blood from her body (actually chocolate syrup) mixes with water and runs down the tub. As it spins around the circular drain, the spinning motion becomes a metaphor for the next shot where Hitchcock introduces a form cut to Marion's eye—which is also slowly turning (canting)—to create one of the most famous form cuts in film history. The shape of an object in one scene (drain) becomes the link to the same shape (eye) in another scene.

18. MONTAGE (several images on a single frame). Montage is commonly defined as several pictures on the same screen. In *Pillow Talk* (1959), Rock Hudson talks on the telephone to Doris Day in a screen montage. In *Woodstock* (1969), several images of the performers are projected onto the same screen at once.

▶ **19. DISSOLVES** (fade in—fade out). This technique occurs when one image slowly fades out into another image or fades to a black screen. The effect is useful in love scenes, soap operas, and to close out a scene.

20. ESTABLISHING SHOT (footage leading to character's first lines). An establishing shot is generally all of the action leading up to the point where the characters begin to talk. *Forest Gump* (1994) opens with a good example of an establishing shot. A feather floats down to the ground during the film credits until it lands in a park and the dialog begins.

21. PARALLEL STORY DEVELOPMENT This screenplay technique suggests the use of jump cuts to allow double narratives. For example, there are two stories going on simultaneously in *Star Wars*—one story is about the Empire, and the other is about the Rebels. The viewer follows one story after the other while jump cuts and wipe lines separate the action of each.

ACTIVITY

A list of film techniques is given below with titles of films, TV programs, or camera techniques that immediately call to mind a particular film technique. For example, a bank security camera typically uses a one-camera shot, while the *Jason Bourne* series conspicuously uses hand-held camera technique. Old cartoon movies often end with the iris-in technique while news broadcasts invariably use the one-camera shot. This list should help you to visualize various film techniques in different film/video contexts.

Break up into groups and select ten film techniques from the list below. Incorporate them into a script for a TV commercial selling toothpaste to a youth audience.

1. Pan (move camera left or right): basketball games, track races, Ping-Pong matches, tennis tournaments, football kickoff, air shows, hockey games, *Saturday Night Fever*.

2. Cant (rotate camera): *Iron Eagle, Top Gun*, sky diving, boats in water, *Wizard of Oz*, roller coasters, *Stargate, Deep Space 9, Men in Black*.

3. Tilt (move camera up and down): NASA spaceship takeoff, *Apollo 13*, view of Empire State Building, bungee jumps, falling objects, *King Kong, Godzilla*.

4. One camera shot (fixed camera) P.O.W., hostage movies, *CNN News Report*, Weather Channel, QVC network, Rush Limbaugh, Court TV, store security cameras.

5. Eye Level Camera Angle (actors' eye level): sitcoms, soap operas, *Star Wars*—cantina scene, *Cheers, Seinfeld, Happy Days*, talk shows.

6. Slanted or Angle Shots (view from above, below, or side): horror movies, *The Birds, Jurassic Park, Dracula*, bronco riding, *Starship Troopers*, and *Frankenstein*.

7. Depth Focus (objects in foreground and background are in focus): *Star Trek*, rock concerts, *Sound of Music, 2001, Lawrence of Arabia*, space battles, IMAX travelogues.

8. Rack Focus (either foreground or background is focused): *Superman, Friday the 13th,* sniper gun scope, soap operas, National Geographic specials.

9. Dolly (zoom) *Vertigo, Wayne's World,* romantic scenes, *Mission Impossible,* rap videos.

10. Track Motion (camera mounted on track): swimming meets, dog races, roller coasters.

11. Truck Motion (camera mounted on a truck): auto races, *Twister,* western cattle drives.

12. Wipe (erase one image with another): *Star Wars, The Sting,* cartoons, *Batman.*

13. Iris in/out (circle closes or opens): silent film technique, *I Love Lucy, Bugs Bunny.*

14. Jump cut (immediate change to new scene): golf tournaments, telephone conversations, *Jumper, Pulp Fiction,* Olympic games, cartoons.

15. Form cut (overlap objects to connect two scenes): *Psycho; 2001, Home Improvement.*

16. Montage (several images on a single frame): *Brady Bunch, Pillow Talk, The Fly,* music videos, news report.

17. Lap Dissolves (overlapping fade in—fade out): soap operas, dream sequences.

18. Establishing shot (footage leading to character's first lines): *Ed Wood, Forest Gump,* and *Contact.*

SOUNDTRACK/MUSIC

Introduction

Music has been a critical part of film making from its beginning—even silent films were viewed to the accompaniment of piano and/or orchestral music. In early nickelodeons, keyboardists improvised musical variations to represent the changing dramatic situations appearing on screen. In major theaters, orchestral players improvised music from cue sheets that were supplied to them with the films. Obviously, the film experience was different for any film in early America because the style and character of music varied at each showing.

One of the first catalogs of music for films was the *Kinothek* (Verlag: *Scheslinger Buchhandlung,* Berlin, 1919–1933) by Giuseppe Becce. This catalog enabled directors to find copyright-free 19th century music to accompany film action. D.W. Griffith's *The Birth of a Nation* (1915) included a hodgepodge of music chosen in this way. It included music by Liszt, Verdi, Beethoven, and even the *Star Spangled Banner.* If a music director could not find appropriate music from the catalog, a composer was hired to write additional music.

One of the important revolutions in film music came with synchronization of film music and images. Director Sergei Eisenstein said that there was a significant correlation between motion in sound and image. He illustrated this theory in *Alexander Nevsky*, a film which included music by Sergei Prokofiev carefully gauged to fit the action. A revolution in sound-image coordination (1967) came in the form of synchronized SMPTE (Society of Motion Picture Television Engineers) codes that involved videotape playback of a film during the final recording. Combining musical temporary tracks with the edited film resulted in a final master that excelled all previous eras of film-making.

FILM MUSIC TYPES

Underscore (Composed Music)

Film underscores are sometimes copied outright from pre-existing compositions such as Samuel Barber's *Adagio for Strings* in *Platoon*, or Mendelsohn's *Symphony No. 3* in *Breaking Away* (1979). More often, however, entirely new compositions are created for a film as in John Williams' music for *Star Wars*. Original film music of this type often aspires to the level of fine art, such as the overtures to *Lawrence of Arabia* or *Dr. Zhivago* (1965). The film industry has created new genres for itself in the opening credits or title cards, such as the *20th Century Fox* logo and the *Cinemascop*e extension. Moreover, the industry has paved the way for audience acceptance of new electronic sounds in science fiction films such as *The Day the Earth Stood Still* (1951) that used *Theremins*, and *Forbidden Planet* (1956) using a specially designed ring modulator. Computer-generated musical orchestrations once unique in films such as *Tron* (1982) are now commonplace in films.

Despite the fact that music is often relegated to the final stage of the filmmaking process, many talented composers have left an indelible mark on the industry. Famous tunes and musical motifs that have helped immortalize films include: *Gone with the Wind* (1939) by Max Steiner, *Love is a Many Splendored Thing* (1955) by Alfred Newman, *Psycho* (1960) by Bernard Hermann, *Lawrence of Arabia* (1962) by Maurice Jarre, *Star Trek* (1979) by Jerry Goldsmith, *Star Wars* (1977) by John Williams, *Batman* (1989) by Danny Elfman, and many others.

MUSIC AS A NARRATOR-ACTOR (*DIEGESIS*)

Music can take on the role of a narrator-actor. In Alfred Hitchcock's *Psycho*, Marion steals $40,000 from her employer and drives off to meet her lover. While driving, she thinks about what people will say when they return to work and discover that she has stolen company money. Tension builds as characters debate with each other in voice-overs about what happened to Marion. A rainstorm begins and water pours down on her car. Marion turns on the windshield wipers and the beat of the music is picked up by the swinging rhythm of the wiper blades. The pounding beat of the music and the synchronized swinging wiper blades carry both the viewer and Marion to the site of her demise—the Bates Motel.

Only music can speak with such intensity at this point in the drama. Words are insufficient and, for thirty seconds, music becomes the narrator-actor (musical diegesis) during the rainstorm sequence.

Foley arts (sound effects) have become increasingly important over the years; careers have been developed in Hollywood based on the ability simply to make unique sounds for films. Consider that the creation of dinosaur sounds in *Jurassic Park* required much thought and exceptional creativity. What sounds would you use to create the atmosphere for a horror film?

Answers spelled backwards: steehsrednuht; sniahc gnilttar; niahc swas; srood gnikaerc; snaom; dniw gnilwoh; etc.

FILM SCRIPT WRITING

Schubert's stand-alone piece entitled *Erlkönig* (*Elfking*)*—one of the masterpieces of 19th century art song literature—contains parallel story development distributed among three actors and a narrator, and all are sung by the same person. The music serves as an excellent example of parallel story development. If you view a performance of this piece online, you may notice that the singer changes her/his posture, gestures like an actor, and changes vocal timbre to match the different characters as the story unfolds. This song is widely available in various performances online.

Elfking is basically a film script that one could write out as shown in Figure **9.3** by screenwriter Britt Morrison. If you plan to submit a film script to producers, and it does not appear exactly as below (i.e., font, typeface, font size, and indentations), it is unlikely that anyone will look at it because the film industry has developed its own special style for film scripts.

♩ PLOT: A man is racing along on a horse carrying his sick son in his arms to get help. They are being chased by the *Elfking* and the whole scene is narrated by a fourth person. The *Elfking* repeatedly breaks into the dialog between the father and his son in an attempt to take the young boy with him. At the tragic end of the song, he takes the boy.

FIGURE 9.3 Source: Elfking *(1815), Franz Schubert. Translation by Steffi Wiggins (2014). Film script adaption by Britt Morrison. © Kendall Hunt Publishing Company.

```
                    "ELFKING"


    FADE IN:


    EXT. FOREST - MOVING - NIGHT


    Galloping on horseback through the forest, a FATHER
    and his sickly CHILD ride like the wind.
```

                    NARRATOR (VO)

Who is riding so late through nightly wind so wild?
It is the father with his child.
He is holding the boy tightly within his arm,
He keeps him safe, he keeps him warm.

                    FATHER
"My son? Why do you hide your face?"

                    CHILD
               (terrified)
"Oh, Father, the Elfking is by your side!
The Elfking with crown and train!"

                    FATHER
               (calming)
"My son, it's only the fog on the plain."

                    ELFKING
               (sweetly)
"Sweet child, come, go with me!
Such pretty games I will play with thee;
On my shore, lovely flowers their blossoms unfold.
My mother's garb is made of gold."

The child tugs on his father's sleeve.

                    CHILD
"Father, oh father, do you not hear what
the Elfking whispers in my ear?"

                    FATHER
"Stay calm, be calm, dear child; T' is only
the wind rustling through the wild."

                    ELFKING
               (beckoning)
"Will you, sweet lad, come with me?
My daughters will care for thee;
At night my daughters their festival keep,
And rock thee and dance thee and sing thee sleep."

                    CHILD
"Oh father, my father, do you not see them there?
The Elfking's daughters are waiting in their lair."

<pre>
                    FATHER
"My son, my son, see what you may,
It is only the ancient willows appearing so grey."

                    ELFKING
"I love thee, I covet thy beauty dear boy;
But if you are not willing, force I'll employ."

                    CHILD
"Father, oh father, he's taking me fast!
The Elfking has harmed me at last."

                  NARRATOR (VO)
The father shudders, runs fast and wild,
His arms clutching his moaning child.
He reaches home with toil and dread,
But in his arms, the child was dead.

                   FADE OUT.
</pre>

*Numerous examples of Schubert's celebrated song are available online.

ACTIVITY

Convert the first paragraph of any short narrative into a script and insert the abbreviations provided below at appropriate places in the dialogue.

SOME SCREENPLAY ABBREVIATIONS:

V.O. = voice over   E.C.U = extreme close-up   EXT. = exterior shot

INT. = interior shot   O.S. = off screen   P.O.V. = point of view

After you have selected a story, try to think about the shots, the camera angles, distance from the actors, and so forth when reducing the story to a screenplay. If you succeed in converting your selection into the format above, you will realize just how difficult it is to write a script and why screenwriters are paid so handsomely for their work. Screenwriting is an attractive, but demanding profession. The screenwriter has to compress the story in such a way that its elements remain intact, but its visual character becomes apparent.

CRITICAL METHOD APPLICATION

Apply the Critical Method to August Wilson's work, *Fences*, starring Denzel Washington and Viola Davis. Remember, as discussed in Chapter One, the steps include Description, Analysis, Interpretation, and Evaluation.

DESCRIPTION

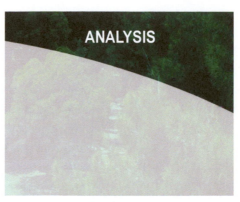
ANALYSIS

INTERPRETATION

EVALUATION

CRITICAL TERMS

TYPES OF FILM

NARRATIVE	Tells a story
DOCUMENTARY	Records actual events or history
EXPERIMENTAL	Exists for its own sake

ELEMENTS OF FILM

PLOT	Story, narrative, and structure of the incidents
FILM TECHNIQUES	Camera, editing, screenplay aspects of organization
SOUND	Vocal, instrumental, and sound effect tracks

ADDITIONAL TERMS

CANT	Rotate camera on lens axis
DEPTH FOCUS	Everything in the shot is in focus
DOLLY	Camera moves in or out on a truck (like zoom)
ESTABLISHING SHOT	Material up to where characters begin to talk
EYE LEVEL ANGLE	Camera is at the eye level of characters
FOLEY ARTS	Sound effects
FORM CUT	Overlap objects to connect two scenes
HAND HELD CAMERA	Camera moves with the film maker
IRIS IN/OUT	Image closes or opens on a circle
JUMP CUT	Immediate change to new scene or point of view
LAP DISSOLVES	One image fades out while another fades in
MONTAGE	Several images in a single frame
MUSICAL DIEGESIS	Music becomes an actor or dominant aspect of the scene
ONE CAMERA SHOT	Camera is locked in position
PAN	Rotate camera on vertical axis
PARALLEL STORY DEVELOPMENT	Two parallel stories maintained by jump cuts.
RACK FOCUS	Either foreground or background is focused
SHOT	A set of images that join together one section in a scene
SLANTED OR ANGLE SHOTS	Odd angles to introduce fear or terror
TILT	Rotate camera on horizontal axis
TRACK MOTION	Camera is mounted on a railroad track
TRUCK MOTION	Camera is mounted on a moving vehicle
UNDERSCORE	Background music composed for the film
WIPE LINES	A moving line erases one image with another

REVIEW QUESTION

Assume that you see a picture of the *Emergency Weather Broadcast* test pattern on the test. This technique would be a good example of:

1. one camera shot
2. canting
3. panning

4. wipe
5. none of the above

Answer spelled backwards: tohs aremac eno

CRITICAL COMMENTARY

Film Techniques tell the history of our most popular American art form since its inception 100 years ago. Terms such as surround sound, *Cinerama*, pit orchestra, and color film all mark points on a timeline of 20th century film history and developments in the art form that enable us to discuss the art form intelligently. Exercises in film criticism can increase the student's ability to write, organize, and evaluate sources.

INDEX

A

Absolute dance, 159
Aesthetics, 7
Affektenlehre, theory of, 127
African tribal dance, 158
Alexander Nevsky, 177
Algeciras, Spain, 132
A-maze-ing Laughter, 64
American Gothic, 25
American Pie, 118
Analogous colors, 20
Anaphora, 128
Ancient Greece, 8
Ancient Greece and lyric
poetry
    Hymn to Aphrodite, 122
    Moon is down, 123
    Sappho's poems, 120–121
Ancient Greek columns, 77
Ancient Greeks, 117–118
Ancient Greek temples
    caryatids, 77
    from the Classical
      period, 75
    floor plan of, 76
    modern pitched roof
      garage, 76
    spread of style of, 79
    triglyphs and metopes, 77
    wall elevation of, 77

Ancient Greek theater
  design, 143
Ancient Rome buildings
  amphitheater, 84–85
  basilica, 83
  bathhouses, 82
  Pantheon, 84
Anikushin, Mikhail, 61
Antitheses, 127
Aphrodite of Melos, 56
Apollo and the Nymphs, 61
Appleseed, Johnny, 135–136
"Arabesque," 162, 163
Architectural techniques, 70
  cantilever, 89–90
  load-bearing wall
    building, 71
  medieval arch, 85–89
  post and lintel
    construction
      Agamemnon palace, 75
      Ancient Greek
        temples, 75–76
      Hephaisteion (Temple
        of *Hephaistos*), 73, 74
      Minoan culture, 73
      Stonehenge at
        Salisbury, 72–73
  Roman arch/vault
    aqueducts, 81–82
    as architectural
      motif, 81

    barrel vault, 81
    basilica, 83
    bathhouses, 82
    centering, 80
    colossal amphitheater,
      84–85
    pozzolan, 81
    ribbing, 81
    at Umm Ar-Rasas, 80
    vault and dome, 81
    without mortar, 81
  skeletal steel frame
    structures, 71–72
Architecture, 65
  elements of
    climate, 70
    context, 69
    importance of, 68–69
    materials, 70
    space/internal
      planning, 69
  government/
    educational, 68
  industrial/
    commercial, 66–67
  residential, 66
  sacred/religious, 67
  vernacular/portable, 68
Aristotle, 147
*Arrangement in Grey and
Black No. 1*, 24

Arrival of the Normandy Train, 29, 37–38

Art
   chairs as, 5–6
   historical definition of, 7
   operational definition of, 5–7

Artistic artifacts, 8

Artworks, 9

Asymmetrical balance, 58–59

Asymmetrical paintings, 24

Atmospheric perspective, 26–27

"Attitude," 162–163

A Valediction Forbidding Mourning, 125

B

Balance, painting, 23–24

Balance, sculpture, 58–59

Balanchine, George, 163

Balashazy, Balint, 97

Ballerina with classic tutu, 162

Ballet comique de la reine, 161

Ballet dance, 127
   "Arabesque," 162
   "Attitude," 162–163
   body positions and movements, 162
   definition of, 160
   feet positions, 161
   Fouetté en tournant, 163
   history of, 161
   moves, 160
   Pavane and *Galliarde,* 161

Barlay, Andras, 97

Baroque poets, 127

Barrel vault, 81

Bartolini, Lorenzo, 7

Basilica, 83

Basilica of Constantine, 83

Bas relief, 44

Baths of Diocletian, 82

Becce, Giuseppe, 176

Berlin Wall fragment, 3

Bernini, Gian Lorenzo, 128

Bird in Space, 55

Birth of a Nation, The, 176

Blasis, Carlo, 162

Bloom, Benjamin, 2

Body positions and movements, 161–162

Bologna, Giovanni, 162

Boone, Daniel, 136

Bound Slaves, 45

Brancusi, Constantin, 55

Breakdance, 158

Brunelleschi, Filippo, 25, 58

Buildings
   aesthetics and function of, 65
   government/educational, 68
   industrial/commercial, 66–67
   residential, 66
   sacred/religious, 67
   vernacular/portable, 68

Buonarroti, Michelangelo, 27, 45

C

Canova, Antonio, 50–51

Cantilever structure
   Marina City, 90

Caro, Sir Anthony, 52

Catharsis, 153

Cathedrals, 85

design features, 89
   floor plan, 86
   flying buttresses, 87
   Gothic, 88
   roof of, 87
   and vaulting, 88

Chiaroscuro, 15

Chord
   cadences, 101
   cluster, 100
   consonant and dissonant triads, 100–101
   definition of, 100
   major and minor, 101

Choreography, 163

Choreology, 163

Clark, Sir Kenneth, 7

Climate, architecture, 70

Closed design, 28

Cloud Gate, 55, 62

Cole, Thomas, 26, 27

Cologne Cathedral, 86

Color, painting, 18–20
   hue, 19
   saturation, 20

Color, sculpture, 53

Color wheel, 20–21

Commercial buildings, 66–67

Complementary colors, 20–21

Conceit, 124–125

Conjunct contour, 98

Conquest of Dacia, 52

Consonant and dissonant triads, 100–101

Context, architecture, 69

Corinthian order, 78

Crashaw, John, 127

Crashaw, Richard, 129

Critical Method
   for art works, 3–5

steps of
    analysis, 3, 4
    description, 3, 4
    evaluation, 3, 5
    interpretation, 3, 4
Culture, 8
Cunningham, Merce, 159
Cupid and Psyche, 51

D

Dali, Salvador, 23, 26
Dance
    absolute, 159
    ballet
        "Arabesque," 162
        "Attitude," 162–163
        body positions and
            movements, 162
        definition of, 160
        feet positions, 161
        Fouetté en tournant, 163
        history of, 161
        moves, 160
        *Pavane and
            Galliarde,* 161
    breakdance, 158
    definition of, 157
    elements of, 160
    narrative, 159
    ritual/healing, 158
David, Jacques-Louis, 13–14
Dazu Rock Carvings, 58–59
Death of Socrates, 13–14
de Beaujoyeaulx,
    Balthazar, 161
Delacroix, Eugène, 33, 36
Deposition, 28
Design analysis, painting, *32*
    hieratic analysis, 36–37

narrative analysis
    *Liberty Leading the
        People,* 33–34
    *Raft of the
        Medusa,* 32, 33
    Wreck of the Hope, 34
    structural analysis, 34–36
        *Liberty Leading the
            People,* 35, 36
        *Raft of the
            Medusa,* 35, 36
        *Wreck of the
            Hope,* 35, 36
Design elements, painting
    color, 18–20
        hue, 19
        saturation, 20
    color wheel, 20–21
    line, 16–17
    shape, 16
    texture, 18
    value, 15
Design principles,
    painting, 21
    balance, 23–24
        asymmetrical, 24
        symmetrical, 23
        radial, 24
    direction, 25
    dominance *vs.*
        subordinance, 30–31
    focal point, 22–23
    linear *vs.* painterly, 28–29
    open *vs.* closed, 27–28
    scale and proportion, 25
    sequence, 30
    space and
        perspective, 25–27
    trick of the eye, 31
    unity, 22
    variety, 22

Direction
    painting, 25
    sculpture, 55
Discipline of Mirth, The, 15
*Disintegration of the
    Persistence of Memory,* 26
Disjunct contour, 99
Documentary film, 169
Dominance *vs.*
    subordinance, 30–31,
    54–55
Donne, John, 125
Doorjambs, 89
Dragon Panel, 44
Drama
    catharsis, 153
    chorus, 145
    definition of, 141
    elements of
        character, 147
        diction, 147
        melody, 148
        plot, 147
        spectacle, 148
        thought, 147
    financial support
        money, 146
        producers, 146
        programs, 147
        publicity/
            advertisements, 146
        tickets, 147
    music, 145
    Oedipus Rex, 149–153
    origin of, 143
    participants, 146
    practical requirements
        for, 142
        costumes, 144
        dressing rooms/
            skene, 143
        lighting, 144

props/machinery, 144

sound system, 144

stage, 143

theater, 143

script, 144–145

Dramatic poetry

definition of, 119

Hamlet, 119

soliloquy, 119

Drawing, techniques of, 18

Dynamic curves, 105

Dynamics

definition of, 104

dynamic curves, 105

polydynamics, 104, 105

terrace, 104

E

Early One Morning, 52

Ecstasy of Santa Teresa, 128

Educational buildings, 68

Eisenstein, Sergei, 177

Entablature, 77, 78

Environment, sculpture, 61

Epic poetry

characteristics of, 135

definition of, 118

legend, 135

Odyssey, 118–119

in Western tradition, 134

Epidauros, 143

Erlkönig, 178–180

Experimental film, 169

Expressed (actual) line, 17

F

Façade with pediment, 78

Falling Water, 66, 90

Fall of the Damned, 18, 19

Family of Saltimbanques, 19, 20

Fast tempo, 102

Figures of speech, 127–130

anaphora, 128

antitheses, 127

metaphor, 127

oxymoron, 127

simile, 128

Film industry, 168

Film music, 177–178

Films

documentary, 169

elements of

film techniques, 170, 171–175

plot, 169

sound, 170

experimental, 169

growth of, 167

history of, 167

narrative, 168

technical advances, 168

United States as leader in, 167

Film script writing, 178–180

Film techniques, 170–175

camera

basic movements, 171

boom mount, 173

cant motion, 172

depth focus, 173

eye level camera angle, 172

hand held camera technique, 174

iris in/out, 173

one camera shot, 172

pan motion, 172

rack focus, 173

slanted or angle shots, 173

tilt motion, 172

track motion, 173

truck motion, 173

zoom, 173

film editing

dissolves, 174

formcut, 174

jumpcut, 174

montage, 174

wipe lines, 174

screenplay, 175

Fine arts, 11

Five Grotesque Heads, 17

Flaming Heart, The, 127–130

Flaming Heart upon the Book and Picture of St. Teresa, The, 127, 128

Flavian Colosseum, 84–85

Focal point, 22–23, 57

Folk art, 9–11

Folk society, 10

Folk values, 10

Fouetté en tournant, 163

Free-standing sculpture, 42–43

Friedrich, Caspar David, 34, 35, 36

G

Gare Sainte Lazare, 29, 38

Gehry, Frank, 66

Geometric shapes, 16, 60

Géricault, Théodore, 32, 33

Giza Pyramids, 67

God Horus, 60

Gothic arches, 87–88

Gothic cathedral, 88

Government buildings, 84

Grand Festival of Russian National Orchestra, 105
Great Wheel, 87–88
Groin vault, 81

H

Haas Haus, 66–67
Hamlet, 119
Hard attack, 113
Harmonic instruments, 112
Harmonic series, 110–111
Harmony, 100
Haut relief, 44
Heterophonic music, 107
Hieratic analysis, 36–37
Hieratic scale, 25
Hieron, floor plan of, 76
Hollein, Hans, 66
Homage to the Square: Apparition, 16
Homophonic music, 106
Humanism, 9
Humanities, 8
Humanities Across the Arts, 8

I

Iliad, 118
Ilyich Tchaikovsky, Pyotr, 163
Implied lines, 17
Indiana, Robert, 51
Industrial buildings, 66–67
Inharmonic instruments, 112
In the Days of Sappho, 22
Ionic order, 78

J

Joyce, James, 131–134

K

Kaufmann, Edgar J., 90
Kinetic sculpture, 43
Kinothek, 176

L

"*Last of the Mohicans, The*," 26
LeBrun, Charles, 127
Legend, 135
Les Sylphides, 159–160
Liberty Leading the People
    narrative analysis, 33–34
    structural analysis, 36
Line, 16–17, 52
Linear perspective, 26
Linear sculpture, 52
Linear *vs.* painterly, 28–29
Long decay, 113
Louvre Museum, 6
Love, 51
Lyric poetry
    ancient Greece
        Hymn to Aphrodite, 122
        Moon is down, 123
        Sappho's poems, 121
    of Ancient Greeks, 117–118
    Baroque era, 127–130
    definition of, 117
    modern poets, 130–134

modernism in literature, 130–131
    stream of consciousness, 131–134
renaissance
    conceit, 124–125
    recitative, 123
    sonnets, 124

M

Madonna of the Meadow, 28
Madonna of the Rocks, 15
Maison Carrée, 79
Major and minor chord, 101
Malakhov, Vladimir, 160
Marin County Courthouse, 68
Materials, architecture, 70
McLean, Don, 118
Medical-religious ritual, 153
Medieval religious paintings, 25
Méliès, George, 167, 168
Melismatic, 99
Melody
    conjunct contour, 98
    disjunct contour, 99
    melismatic, 99
    pitches, 98
    syllabic, 99
Metaphor, 127
Methode pour apprendre à dessiner les passions, 127
Modern poets, 130–134
    modernism in literature, 130–131
    stream of consciousness, 131–134
"Mollie's Monologue," 132–134
Mona Lisa, 6

Monet, Claude, 29

Monophonic music, 106

Monument to the Heroic Defenders of Leningrad, 61

Mount Rushmore, 46

Mural painting, 17

Music, 95–96

    elements of. *See* Music, elements of

Music, elements of, 97

    chord

        cadences, 101

        cluster, 100

        consonant and dissonant triads, 100–101

        definition of, 100

        major and minor, 101

    dynamics

        definition of, 104

        dynamic curves, 105

        polydynamics, 104, 105

        terrace, 104

    harmony, 100

    melody

        conjunct contour, 98

        disjunct contour, 99

        melismatic, 99

        pitches, 98

        syllabic, 99

    rhythm

        definition of, 102

        fast tempo, 102

        non-pulse, 102

        pulse, 102

        rubato, 103

        slow tempo, 102

    texture

        blend, 108

        density, 107–108

        heterophonic, 107

        homophonic, 106

        monophonic, 106

        polyphonic, 106–107

        range, 109

        register, 108–109

    timbre

        definition of, 110

        harmonic series, 110–111

        harmonic sounding instruments, 112

        inharmonic or noisy instruments, 112

        waveform envelope, 112–113

Musicology, 97

Myth, 136

N

Narrative analysis

    Liberty Leading the People, 33–34

    Raft of the Medusa, 32, 33

    Wreck of the Hope, 34

Narrative dance, 159

Narrative film, 168

Nefertiti, 53

Night and Fog, 169

Noisy instruments, 112

Non-pulse, 102

Non-western instrumentation, 113

Notre-Dame d'Amiens Cathedral, 88–89

Nude: A Study in Ideal Form (Doubleday Anchor), *The,* 7

Nude *vs.* naked, 7

Nymph with Scorpion, 7

O

Odyssey, 118–119

Oedipus Rex, 149–153

    background, 149–151

    plot structure in, 151–153

Old Guitarist, 30, 31

Oleksiy, Fedorov, 13

On Poetry, 147

Open design, 27

Open planning, 90

Open *vs.* closed, 27–28, 58

Organic shapes, 16

Outhouse Society of America, 68

Oxymoron, 127

P

Painterly *vs.* linear, 28

Paintings, 13–15

    design elements

        color, 18–20

        color wheel, 20–21

        line, 16–17

        shape, 16

        texture, 18

        value, 15

    design principles, 21

        balance, 23–24

        direction, 25

        dominance *vs.* subordinance, 30–31

        focal point, 22–23

        linear *vs.* painterly, 28–29

        open *vs.* closed, 27–28

        scale and proportion, 25

        sequence, 30

space and
perspective, 25–27
trick of the eye, 31
unity, 22
variety, 22
Pantheon, 84
Parthenon, 78
Pavane and *Galliarde,* 161
Pei, I. M., 66
Persistence of Memory, 26
Personages with Stars, 16
Piano keyboard, 96
Picasso, Pablo, 30
Pitches, 98
Plot, 169
definition of, 147
structure of, 148
Poetics, 147
Poetry
dramatic
definition of, 119
Hamlet, 119
soliloquy, 119
epic
characteristics of, 135
definition of, 118
legend, 135–136
and myth, 136
Odyssey, 118–119
in Western
tradition, 134
lyric
ancient Greece
Hymn to
Aphrodite, 122
Moon is down, 123
Sappho's poems,
120–121
of Ancient Greeks,
117–118
Baroque era, 127–129
definition of, 117

modern poets, 130–134
renaissance, 124–126
Sonnet No. 18, 120
Polydynamics, 104, 105
Polyphonic music, 106–107
Pont du Gard, 82
Porch of Caryatids, 77
Portable buildings, 68
*Portrait of a Man with a
Golden Helmet,* 22–23
*Principles of Art
History,* 27, 58
Proportion, sculpture, 56
Pulse, 102

Q

QUINTA Orchestra, 100

R

Radial balance, 58–59
Radial design, 24
Raft of the Medusa, 32
narrative analysis, 32, 33
structural analysis, 36
Reagan, Ronald, 2
Recitative, 123
Recognition scenes, 152
Red Cube, 60
Relief sculpture, 44
Religious buildings, 67
Renaissance, 8–9
and lyric poetry
conceit, 124–125
recitative, 123
sonnets, 124
Renaissance art, 27
Residential buildings, 66

Reversals, 148
Rhythm
definition of, 102
fast tempo, 102
non-pulse, 102
pulse, 102
rubato, 103
slow tempo, 102
Rinascimento, 8
Ritual/healing dance, 158
Roman Basilica floor
plan, 83
Rubato, 103

S

Sacred buildings, 67
Sacrifice of Isaac, 58
Sanzio, Raphael, 28
Scale and proportion, 25
Schubert, Franz, 178–180
Sculptural methods
addition/assemblage, 46
modeling, 47–48
readymades, 49–50
substitution/
casting, 47
subtraction/
carving, 45–46
temporary
installations, 48–49
Sculpture, 41–42
design elements
color, 53
line, 52
shape, 51
space/volume, 53–54
texture, 52
value, 50–51
design principles
balance, 58–59

direction, 55

dominance *vs.* subordinance, 54–55

environment, 61

focal point, 57

open *vs.* closed, 58

proportion, 56

sequence, 56–57

unity, 60

variety, 61

free-standing, 42–43

kinetic, 43

relief, 44

Self-Portrait, 17, 19, 30, 31

Sequence, 30, 56–57

Shakespeare and Company, 131

Shakespearean sonnet rhyme scheme, 124

Shakespeare, William, 119–120, 123–124

Shape, 16, 51

Simile, 128

Single note, attack and decay character of, 112

Slow tempo, 102

Smithson, Robert, 57

Soft attack, 113

Soliloquy, 119

Sonnets, 124

Sophocles, 149–151

Sound, 170

South Rose window, 24

Space and perspective, 25–27

Space/internal planning, architecture, 69

Space/volume, 53–54

Sphinx and Khafre Pyramid, 67

Spiral Jetty, 57

Starry Night, The, 2–5

Star Wars, 134–135

Statue of Liberty, 54

St. John of the Cross, 23

Structural analysis, 34–36

Liberty Leading the People, 36

Raft of the Medusa, 36

Wreck of the Hope, 36

Studia humanitatis, 8

Subordinance *vs.* dominance, 54–55

Sullivan, Louis, 65

Sunken relief, 44

Surface texture, 18

Syllabic, 99

Sylvia Beach's original bookstore, 131

Symmetrical balance, 58–59

Symmetrical paintings, 23

T

Temple of Horus, 60

Terme di Diocleziano, 82

Terrace, 104

Texture, 18, 52

blend, 108

density, 107–109

heterophonic, 107

homophonic, 106

monophonic, 106

polyphonic, 106–107

range, 109

register, 108–109

Thespis, 146

Timbre

definition of, 110

harmonic series, 110–111

harmonic sounding instruments, 112

inharmonic or noisy instruments, 112

waveform envelope, 112–113

Trajan's Column, 52

Transfiguration on Mount Tabor, 37

Trick of the eye, 31

Triumph of the Will, 169

Trompe l'oeil. See Trick of the eye

U

Ulysses, 131–134

Underscores, 177

Unity, 22, 60

Urban art

and fine arts, 11

urban values, 11

V

Value, 15, 50–51

van Gogh, Vincent, 3–5, 18–19

van Rijn, Rembrandt, 30, 31

Variety, 22, 61

Venus de Milo. See Aphrodite of Melos

Vernacular buildings, 68

Virgin and Child Enthroned, The, 25

Virgin of the Rocks, The, 30

Visual texture, 18

W

Water Lilies, 20, 21
Western culture
    definition of, 8
    timeline of, 8–9
Western tradition, epic
    poetry in, 134
Wheel of Life, The, 58–59
Whistler, James McNeil, 24
Wölfflin, Heinrich, 27, 58
Wreck of the Hope
    narrative analysis, 34
    structural analysis, 36
Wright, Frank Lloyd, 90

Y

Yoshioka, Mika, 160